PROLOGUE

TO THE ENGLISH EDITION

This book is about what happens to us when we die; from the moment of death onwards.

This is an age of half-truths, 'faction' and blatant lies, of cynicism and scepticism, when so much of what we are told or are led to believe is false or, at best, uninformed speculation. It is, therefore, extremely important to know the real and actual Truth - to be able to distinguish it from that which is not.

And when the subject touches on that which will be ours for ever, eternally, then it is clearly of paramount importance that we know the truth.

As Fr. Alexander Schmemann says:

"Truth is the criterion. The purpose of Christianity is not to help people by reconciling them with death, but to reveal the Truth about life and death in order that people may be saved by this Truth...

Christ is this Life. And only if Christ is Life is death what Christianity proclaims it to be, namely the enemy to be destroyed and not a mystery to be explained"[1].

Jesus said: "*I am the Way, Truth and Life*" *(John 14:6)*. His words are true. And if we follow His commandments in all humility, with love and faith in Him, then we shall of a certainty inherit Life eternal in Him.

Moreover, He Himself has told us something of that which can and something of that which will happen to us after death. We have only to read *(Luke 16:19-31)* about the rich man and Lazarus, the poor beggar. We learn there how the angels took Lazarus to a place of comfort, but that the rich man found himself in torment in Hades.

And if we turn to Matthew *(25:30-46)*, Christ tells us the essential details of the Last Judgement.

Finally there are Christ's words to the Good Thief, as He hung on the cross: "*Truly I say to you, today you will be with Me in Paradise*".

All this should be enough to convince us. But, weak as we are, the power of Christ's words are often of little avail. Even His disciples, who were eye-witnesses of His life and crucifixion, were unwilling to believe in the Resurrection until they had evidence from beyond the grave - the physical presence of the Risen Lord. God, in His ineffable goodness and fathomless love for each of us, has continued to provide such evidence for us down the ages, through Christ Himself and the Saints.

St. Mark the Ascetic says "*The first among all evils is ignorance*", a position with which St. Theodore of Jerusalem and Syria, the great ascetic, concurs wholeheartedly:

---

1. For the Life of the World, p. 99.

To,
My dear Mrs Olga
with
Christ's love
Maria

AFTER DEATH

And this book is very-very interesting
good reading.

AFTER DEATH

by
Father Vasilios Bakogiannis
B. Theol. University of Belgrade,
M. Theol. St. Vladimir's Seminary.

English Translation
by
W.J. Lillie

2nd edition

TERTIOS Publications

"AFTER DEATH"
Written by: Archim. Vasilios Bakogiannis
Translated into English by: W. J. Lillie
© TERTIOS - Archim. Vas. Bakogiannis
ISBN (English edition): 960-7297-92-X
1st English edition: September 1995
2nd English edition: April 2001
DTP by TERTIOS

TERTIOS Publications, C. Papagiannoulis and Co.
2nd km Katerini - N.Keramidi rd
GR-601 00 Katerini, HELLAS
Tel.: (351) 22098 - Fax: (351) 45815

PROLOGUE

by the RT. REVD. METROPOLITAN
NIKODEMOS OF PATRAS.

The interest of the human race has from the first been directed towards the vital question:

"What happens after death?"

For this reason, it is most useful to have the treatment of the subject undertaken through this book by the Very Reverend Archimandrite Vasilios Bakogiannis, one of the highly-educated members of the clergy of our Holy Metropolis.

The "beyond" has exercised both philosophers and the popular imagination. On a world-wide scale, throughout the centuries, the diversity of religions has been accompanied by a diversity of views concerning the final issue of human personality.

A certain core of the scriptural truth concerning eternal life has indeed been preserved in the multifarious beliefs of peoples and nations, and this truth also emerges, to some degree, from the depths of human consciousness. It is certain, however, that only in the light of the Gospel of Christ and from the point of view of Patristic wisdom, enlightened by God and taught by Christ, is this great universal problem

5

unimpeachably and authoritatively illumined.

Thus, the author of the present book, using these parameters and criteria in his analysis of the problem, and employing a simple and engaging manner, presents the reader with the Christian teaching on this matter, especially the treasures of the Orthodox teaching of the Holy Fathers (Niptic and others), in order to consider the subject in a constructive, "certain and sure" manner.

This being so, we bless the endeavour, in order that, by the Lord's grace, it may prove instructive and spiritually profitable to the people of the Lord.

The Fervent Intercessor

NIKODEMOS,
METROPOLITAN OF PATRAS,

15.1.1989

"*Indeed, ignorance is the root of all evils*". In view of which, Father Vasilios has rendered us all a great service by bringing together so much valuable information, all of it from unimpeachable Orthodox sources. Some of it we may find unpalatable, but we cannot pick and choose. Father Vasilios has also included many important details of how the Church helps and cares for the departing and departed soul as it makes its crucial journey.

Combining as he does a style which is both easy to read and disarmingly direct, the author is able to present us with a very clear and intelligible account of his subject, for which he deserves our warmest congratulations and heartfelt thanks.

Ann Lillie
Panorama, Thessaloniki
Bright Monday 1993.

1. ON ETERNAL LIFE

1. Man's weakness.

"Many are the wonders, but none so wonderful as Man" *(Sophocles, Antigone, v.332)*. Indeed, many are the wonderful things in this world, but the most wonderful of all is Mankind. We ourselves are magnificent creations as are many of our works. But since we see them every day, they do not impress us. Familiarity breeds contempt. For example: the motor car is a great and complex invention but since we are now used to it, it no longer impresses us. The same holds true for the train, the telephone, the radio, television, aeroplanes, spaceships, the computer and so on.

Now why all this? God gave Mankind a gift: the brain. And with this gift, Mankind has created this astonishing civilisation. Which is why it is not Mankind who should be praised for having done so, but rather God, Who made us a gift of such magnitude and importance.

But although people have within them such a great gift, with such great power, they have nothing to say about a few simple phenomena. They are unable to comprehend or explain them. Their brains cannot cope.

How is it, for instance, that sheep give birth every year to male and female offspring? Why not only to males?

Or only females? But males and females? Why is it that the almond tree blossoms in January or February? Why doesn't it do so in December. Or March? How can it tell the months apart? And why does the almond tree produce all almonds? Why not also walnuts? Or why not a thousand almonds and one walnut. How does it manage it?

And this is particularly odd:

We, who have brains, make mistakes in the work we do every day. The almond tree, which does not have a brain, and which does not work every day but only once a year, does not make any mistakes! What explanation do people, with their mighty brains, give for that?

But the world does not consist only of sheep and almonds and nothing else. It consists of thousands upon thousands of species. And each one of them has its own enigma, its own inexplicable mystery. As for the specialist scientists whose job it is to investigate Nature and the Universe, their brains are thrown into a whirl and they are left speechless. Even atheist scientists raise their hands in surrender and say: "*These are inexplicable phenomena. Of necessity, God the Creator exists!*".

What does all this mean to us? The following, which is worth noting:

People are unable properly to comprehend this perceptible world, which they see and hear and which acts on their feelings. So how can they seek to understand eternal life, which does not do so? They cannot understand the visible, so how can they understand the invisible? They do not understand the perceptible so how can they understand the imperceptible? They do not understand the bee, so how can they understand God. Or Eternal Life? And yet they insist on comprehending the incomprehensible: the mysteries of God. Who? Those who do not understand the mysteries of the bee.

2. *"Has anyone come from above?"*

Many people ask: "*Has anyone ever come from above to tell us what happens?* ". The answer is: "*Yes*" And not just one, but many!

1. Jess E. Weiss wrote a book of great moment, "*The Vestibule*".

In this book there are descriptions of cases of people who were clinically dead. Their souls left their bodies. And went to the next world. They then returned. And the people came back to life! And spoke about what they saw. Some of them, in fact, were atheists and repented. They became Christian.

2. And how many such cases do we hear about every day, but are not mentioned, either on the radio or television...

3. Those who most regularly visit us from the next world, however, are the saints with their miracles.

The saints were people such as we are. Saint Nektarios was, for example, just like us. He was seen. He had a body and soul. He ate, slept, walked. He grew old, fell ill and went to hospital. He died. He was buried in the ground. His body became dust. But how many miracles Saint Nektarios performs! He is continually doing so. And that means that the saint is still alive. What can a dead person do? Or perhaps all these miracles are the result of auto-suggestion?

Is a miracle the result of auto-suggestion?

• Is it auto-suggestion that keeps water which has been blessed from going off?

• Is it by auto-suggestion that the body of Saint Spyridon "*has lain uncorrupted*" for about one thousand six hundred years?

• Is it auto-suggestion that makes the candle-lamp of the Most Holy Mother of God move by itself at the Monastery of Iviron on Mount Athos?

• At Easter, the light at the Most Holy Tomb of Christ springs forth by itself from a marble slab. Is the marble slab subject to auto-suggestion?

It is nonsense for us to believe that miracles are the result of auto-suggestion.

Therefore the fact that Saint Nektarios performs miracles means:

a. that he is alive; therefore, eternal life exists, and

b. that whoever dies passes over into the next life. Precisely because Saint Nektarios was a man just like us.

3.What is eternal life like?

a. Everyone has thoughts about eternal life, Paradise and Hell. But whatever people imagine, it is not eternal life, because it is based on earthly experiences and thoughts and imaginings. Nor can it be otherwise. Therefore for us who live on earth in the flesh, eternal life remains a mystery.

b. Saul (later the Apostle Paul) "*was blinded*" when he beheld the Lord of Glory. Because he was unworthy. And we, too, "*are blinded*" when we gaze upon eternal life, because we are unworthy. But when the Apostle Paul was cleansed and sanctified, he himself, who previously had

had no idea, reveals to us the mysteries of eternal life *(I Corinthians 13, 12 and II Corinthians 12, 4)*.

Another who was well-versed in these matters, Saint Symeon the New Theologian tells us: Let us suppose that someone is in prison. And in the dark. He sees nothing outside: not the outside world, trees, streets, people, the sun. But if there is a crack in the prison, and a little light gets in, that is enough for him to make out the world out- side to some extent and to wonder at it! But when he has been set free for good and come out of the prison and is in the light of the sun, then he sees and admires everything. We, too, says Saint Symeon, are imprisoned by the pas- sions, in the dark. And because of this, we have no idea about eternal life. Once we escape from the prison of the passions, the darkness, and enter the Light of Christ, then in this Light we shall see eternal life and wonder at it *(Τά Εύρισκόμενα, p. 231)*.

So long as we have no idea about eternal life, we ought humbly to be taught by those who do have knowledge and experience of it. And they are the saints, who have been released from the prison of the passions. Let us not fumble about by ourselves in the dark, without light.

God Himse lf promises: "*I shall give you hidden treasures*" *(Isaiah 45, 3)*. And He fulfils His promise. He re- veals his "*secrets*" to his humble servants. The experience of Saint John of the Ladder speaks about this. The perfect servant of God is "...*an abyss of knowledge, a dwelling-place of mysteries*" *(The Ladder, Logos 26, ibid.)*. As does the expe- rience of Saint Gregory of Sinai: just as we read books, so do the saints read the next world. The book is the Holy Spirit; their ink, the Light; their pen the intellect "*My tongue is the pen of a ready writer"* (Psalm 44, 2)[2].

We are told roughly about what eternal life is like by the following incident. It occurred to a prominent physician, Gennadios by name, who was a contemporary of Saint Augustine. Saint Augustine himself tells us:

Gennadios was a materialist. He did not believe in God, nor in the soul. Nor in immortality, nor Hell. Nor in angels, nor devils. And he was proud of that.

One night while he was asleep, Gennadios had a dream. A young man appeared at the side of his bed. It seemed to Gennadios that it might have been him who woke him up. And he said to him: *"Follow me"*.

Gennadios willingly arose and followed him. They walked along together for some time, through beautiful places, until they reached a town where they heard wonderful music.

Gennadios awoke at peace. He had enjoyed the adventure, but as the materialist he was, he paid no attention to it. *"Pity"*, he said. *"It was just a dream!"*

Quite a long time passed from then. And then, all at once he sees that same young man standing beside him in a dream and asking: *"Do you know me, Gennadios?*

- I remember you extremely well.

- What do you remember?

- I remember that you once came and we went together to a town where we heard wonderful music.

- How did you see that town? How did you hear that

2. All psalms are numbered as in the Septuagint Bible, in accordance with Orthodox practice. Translator's note.

music? Were you awake or dreaming?

- Dreaming!

- Where was your body?

- In bed.

- Your eyes were open or closed?

- Closed.

- Did you see me?

- I saw you.

- Did you hear me?

- I heard you.

- Then how did you see me. With what eyes? And with what ears did you hear me and the music?"

The doctor did not know what to answer, and then the young man said to him:

"You see. Even though your eyes were closed, your senses inert and your body drugged by sleep and motionless, you live and act and have enjoyable adventures. You have a life independent of the body. The same happens after death, too. You'll see with other eyes and hear with other ears. And you'll live without the body. So stop doubting that there is another life".

Gennadios awoke and wanted to say again that it was a dream. But he could not. This time he wondered: "Was it a dream or instruction?"

He was unable to give a definite answer, but from that time on he began to believe. Gennadios himself, a Christian by now, told this story to Saint Augustine.

4. We live Life.

How is life to be understood? How is life felt? By living it! When we live, we already have life.

Eternal life is Life. It is therefore felt, understood when we live eternal life. And this happens with the sacraments of the Church, especially with that of Holy Communion. The Lord Himself said: *"Truly, truly I say to you, unless you eat the flesh of the Son of Man and drink His blood, you have no life in you"* (John VI, 53). And when the Lord says life, He does not mean biological life, which they already had, but eternal life. *"Whoever eats my flesh and drinks my blood has eternal life"* (ibid.).

Whoever, therefore, does not live the sacramental life has no feeling for life, i.e. eternal life. And ends up denying it.

2. DEATH

1. Oblivion.

Ionesco, the Franco-Romanian dramatist, was invited in 1972 to make the opening address at a music festival in Austria. Amongst other things, he said: "*We have become oblivious to the main problem of our being, the problem of death. The final end has been banished from our thought, because we have only immediate goals before us.... We do not know what it is we ought to be doing, nor where we should be going. Since all we want is to go on living, our life has become unlivable*". And that is indeed so. "*We have become oblivious to the main problem of our being*". And our brains have become puffed up. Our imaginations, too. And we've taken off. We are no longer rooted in reality, which is death. We're unrealistic. We live and think as if death did not exist!

What are we waiting for? Our death! All of us. Without exception. Even young children! Nobody has a contract with life for an extension. It is open-ended, and the closing date is not known. So death is not a sudden event, since we expect it!

And it's absurd that while people are continually confronted with death, and that others are continuously dying all around them, they are not set thinking in the least about life and about death! Because they are held fast by the pleasures of this world. In this way, their talents, their intellect and their logic have been buried. And they will be punished for this by God.

Everybody knows that they will die. It follows that they do, indeed, think about it, but without undue concern. Because they have not really digested the fact that they will die. It is one thing to think that you will die and quite another to "*take this on board*". Proof? We, too, know that we will die, yet we think and live as if we were never going to! So our lives are artificial. "*He philosophises about death and affects immortality*" *(The Ladder of Saint John of Sinai, Logos XVII, 3).*

On the other hand, those who have really digested the fact that one day they will die are shaken to the very depths of their beings. Saint John of Sinai relates:

"*And I shall not omit to present you with the story of Hesychios the Chorebite. He lived in utter heedlessness, without the slightest care for his soul. Then one day it happened that he fell seriously ill, so seriously, in fact, that at one stage he thought he had died. But he recovered and begged us all to leave at once.*

Then he bricked up the door to his cell and stayed there for twelve years as a recluse, without speaking to anyone. In all this time, he tasted nothing but bread and water. He simply sat enraptured before that which he had seen in his ecstasy. So rapt in thought that his expression no longer changed. And all the time abstracted, shedding silent, warm tears continuously.

Only when the hour of his death approached did we

unblock the door and go in. Despite our fervent entreaties, the only thing he said was: 'Forgive me, brethren'. He who knows what it is to bear death in mind can no longer sin". (The Ladder, Logos VI, 20).

The same thing happened to the Emperor of Byzantium, Isaak I Komnenos. One afternoon he went out for a walk. The sky clouded over and it started to rain. Lightning flashed and he ran for shelter. One flash of lightning struck the earth very close to him. This shook him and he said: "I saw how close death is! And what do I do for my soul?. Nothing". He went back to the palace and abdicated! He went to a monastery and became a monk. The monastery door-keeper!

A real awareness of death, then, devastates people. It brings them down to earth, makes them realists. This is why Saint Isaak the Syrian, with his clear, philosophical mind, tells us: "The really sensible and astute person is the one who understands properly that there is an end to the present life and who makes haste to put an end to his errors and failings. For what knowledge or discretion is greater than this, that is for someone to contrive to quit this life for eternity, without having been corrupted by sin, without any of their members having been sullied by the stench of the desires of this world and without their soul having been polluted by this world's apparent and external sweetness". (Εὐεργετινός, vol. IV, p. 325, 2)

2. Why is the hour of death unknown?

No-one knows when they will die. That knowledge belongs solely to God. And God, if and when He wants, discloses it to His servants. Nevertheless, this veil around death is part of God's providence. "*Some of the faithful*", writes Saint John of Sinai, "*question this and want to learn why it is that, since the remembrance of death is so beneficial to us, God hides the hour from us. What they fail to understand is that, in precisely this manner, God achieves our salvation! Because no-one would come to baptism or to the monastic state straight away if they knew the time of their death. They would spend all the days of their lives in sin, and only when the hour of their death approached would they hasten to be baptised and repent.*

But by then they would have become entrenched in wickedness, from long practice, and would be completely incorrigible". (*Saint John of Sinai, ibid. Logos VI, 10*).

The veil surrounding death is also part of God's providence for the following reason: if people knew when they were going to die, they would die before their time! Their lives, awaiting the terrible moment of death, would be bitter. As bitter as gall. Unbearable. So much so that it is doubtful if they would carry out their religious obligations.

No matter how strong a person is, how much a saint, they do not have the strength, the resources to face the terror of death unless God intervenes. If Christ, Who was God, was cast down by death, and interrupted His prayer to seek comfort from His disciples *(Matthew 26, 40-41)*, then what can an ordinary person do? Even if he or she is a saint. And what about the sinners?

3. Is death accidental?

The following occurred in America: Somebody decided to hang himself from the bridge over a river. He tied the rope to the railings on the bridge, put the noose round his neck and jumped off. As he fell, he thought something might happen and he would not be hanged, so he put a pistol to his head and aimed at his temple. The bullet went through the knot of the noose, however, and cut the rope. Directly underneath, on the water of the river, a small boat was passing, into which he fell-and was saved! *"Are not two sparrows sold for a penny? And not one of them will fall to the ground without your father's will. Do not fear, therefore; you are of greater value than many sparrows"* (Matthew 10, 29-32).

Christ said: *"Even all of the hairs of your head are numbered"* (Matthew 10, 30). So if all the hairs of our heads are numbered in some way, under the Lord's supervision, how much more must the days of our lives be! If not even a hair falls and is lost without the Lord being aware of it, without His consent, how much truer must that be about people! God does nothing injudiciously. Whatever He does, He does in prudence and judgement, even if, to us, most of His judgements are unintelligible. That is what an angel of the Lord told Saint John the Merciful. *"Where God has put a full stop, don't you put a question mark"*, said a sage.

The question is: What are God's thoughts about the death of a person? For instance, we know that babes-in-arms, if they are baptised and die, go to Heaven. God, Who is all-knowing, is aware of who will go to Heaven and who to Hell. So why does He allow those people who will go to Hell to grow up in the first place and not take them at once, as soon as they have been baptised? Why does He send some straight to Paradise, by taking them as babies, and let others burn in Hell? Why does He take some (the babies) and leave others? Does God have *"preferences"*?

Such questions are logical and human. That is as far as our brains get, no further. They cannot. What is it that we are demanding? To understand God's thinking? We can't even understand the thinking of our fellow-men very well, so how can we understand that of God? If the extremely clear mind of the Apostle Paul, the mouth of God, was baffled by God's judgements, what can our own mind do? "*Oh, the depths of the riches and wisdom and knowledge of God! How unsearchable are His judgements and inscrutable His ways!*" (Romans 11 33). Because the Almighty Lord says: "*For my thoughts are not your thoughts, neither are your ways my ways, says the Lord. For as the heavens are higher than the earth, so are my ways higher than your ways and my thoughts than your thoughts*" (Isaiah 55 8-10).

Therefore let us, too, sing with the hymnographer: "*In the depths of Your judgements, Christ, with fullness of wisdom You have pre-ordained the end of each person's life, its appointed time and its manner*" (Triodion, Matins for the Saturday before Meat-fare Sunday, ode I).

The thinking of the Lord may be incomprehensible, but it is still charitable. It contains the depths of charity. "*You, only Creator, who order everything out of love for mankind in the depths of Your wisdom, and apportion what is best to everyone*" (Triodion, Saturday of All-Souls). Not just with wisdom, but in the depths of wisdom. And, moreover, wisdom imbued with charity. "*And apportion what is best to all*". Not to some, but to all! "*All is governed by the goodness of the Lord*" (Basil the Great, Epistle 101). And so God takes each one at the most appropriate moment. He burned Sodom and Gomorah because he saw that in the souls of the people there the very last spark of repentance had died.

Had they lived any longer, they would have spent an even worse time in Hell, and, moreover, the evil would have been compounded. It was in their best interests to die.

Saint Basil the Great teaches on this: "*Now consider that God, Who made us and breathed life into us, has given to each soul a particular way of life and appointed for each a different quietus. Because for some He has arranged that they remain in the body for a greater length of time, while others, according to the undisclosed workings of His wisdom and justice, He releases swiftly from the bonds of the body. Just as with those who are thrown into prison. Some remain locked up in gaol and tormented for a long period of time, while others are quickly set free from hardship. It is the same with souls. Some are kept alive for a long time, others for less, depending on the worth of each. For God Who made us in wisdom and in our depths, deeper than the human mind can reach, foresees everything which concerns each one of us*" (*Homily on the martyr Julita, 5*).

The witness of the martyrs is very revealing. God, for example, protected Saint Eleftherios from many dreadful tortures. From a bed of coals, a grid over coals, boiling pitch, a copper furnace, ravening lions. In the end, Saint Eleftherios was beheaded. God could have stayed the executioner so that the saint would not have been beheaded, as He had done with, for instance, the ravening lions. His unsearchable wisdom, however, deemed that for the saint this was the most appropriate way of departing this world. "*In the depths of Your undisclosed wisdom You order life, and foresee the future, and lead Your servants to an abode in the next life*" (*Paracletic, tone 8, aposticha of the praises for Saturday*).

3. VIOLENT DEATH

1. Erasure of sins.

The Gospel relates the following incident: *"There were some present at that very time who told him of the Galileans whose blood Pilate had mingled with their sacrifices. And he answered them, 'Do you think that these Galileans were worse sinners than all the other Galileans, because they suffered thus? I tell you, No; but unless you repent you will all likewise perish. Or those eighteen upon whom the tower in Siloam fell and killed them, do you think that they were worse offenders than all the others who lived in Jerusalem? I tell you, No; but unless you repent, you will all perish thus'"* (Luke 13, 1-5).

There are many meanings hidden in the words of the Lord. We shall confine ourselves here to the following. The Lord links un-repentance with violent death. *"Unless you repent you will all likewise perish"* (verse 3). *"Unless you repent you will all perish thus"* (verse 5). And the Lord is quite categorical: *"You will all perish likewise"* (verse 3) and *"You will all perish thus"* (verse 5). Not some, but all. Without exception. Compulsory for everyone. *"All".*

The Lord does not have any outstanding scores to settle with any sinner, so as to feel any satisfaction at their tragic death. There is in Him no revenge, no satisfaction. Because there is no animosity. The Lord is not like people, who, when they have "*a bone to pick*" with someone, are happy when something bad happens to that person, because there is animosity. The Lord is all Love.

So when He says you will all perish likewise, He says so out of love. And "*for the Lord reproves whom He loves; He chastises every child whom He acknowledges*" (Proverbs 3, 12). And it is because He loves all mankind that He says "*you will all perish likewise*".

Here the Lord links unrepentance with violent death. By this, He shows that to some extent violent death substitutes for repentance. As if the Lord were saying: "*If it is your intention to go to Hell, I shall find a way of getting you to Paradise. Or if it is your intention to go to the depths of Hell, I shall find a way of ensuring that this does not happen*". And since the Lord "*desires to save all men*" (I Timothy 2, 4) and wants the good of all people, this is why He declares categorically "*you will all perish thus*".

In the lives of the saints, it is recorded that four priests once decided to live together as monks in the desert. They set themselves the aim of being together as a company in heaven as they were on earth. Two of them died, however. And their souls went to Paradise. One day, one of the two brothers, went to the town on an errand. And there he fell into debauchery! The Devil created turmoil within him and darkened his thoughts and would not allow him to return to the place of his repentance. Finally, however, he took the road back. The souls of his brothers, who were in Paradise, followed him. And they could tell that it would be difficult for him to repent. They begged God that their brother, who had sinned, should die a violent death, so that his sin would be forgiven and he could be with them in the Kingdom of God. And God heard their prayers. He sent a ravening lion to tear him to pieces. The other brother, however, who was in the desert, was told by God about the plight of his brother.

He heard the growling of the lion and was greatly agitated. His brother was in danger! At once he fell on his knees and implored God to deliver his brother. Now behold: three brothers were praying for their brother. Two were entreating God for the lion to tear him to pieces and the other for him to be delivered. So what does the lion do? It takes a run at the brother. It gets there, goes right up to him, and leaps to tear him limb from limb. Then suddenly makes a peculiar twist and disappears. God heard the prayer of the brother who was still alive. Because had the other brother died, then he would have been left all alone on earth, without consolation, while the others in Paradise would have had the consolation of Paradise itself. *(Εὐεργετινός vol. III, pp. 504-5)*

So the souls in Paradise prayed for their brother to have a violent death. And God was perfectly willing to countenance such a prayer. Conclusion: violent death cleanses the soul. It achieves forgiveness of sins, as does sickness *(I Corinthians 11, 32)*. There is some truth in the expression "*Kill me so that I can go to Paradise*".

2. Violent death and the righteous.

"*Do you think that these Galileans were worse sinners than all the other Galileans because they suffered thus? Or those eighteen upon whom the tower in Siloam fell and killed, do you think that they were worse offenders than all the* others *who dwelt in Jerusalem? I tell you, No"*. *(Luke 13, 2-5)*. It is, therefore, not only sinners who die violent deaths, but the righteous, too. *(Εὐεργετινός, vol. III, pp. 233-243)*.

a. Forgiveness of their offences.

Tragic death erases sins. The righteous, too, being people, have offended. Which is why the Lord permits their tragic death. The prophet Achia, because he transgressed the Lord's command, was punished by Him. A lion took away his life. And he did not return to the land of his fathers. The lion only took away his life, however; it did not tear him apart!

And it stayed there, guarding the prophet's ass and his dead body. So by his tragic death the prophet expunged his disobedience *(1 Kings, chapter 13)*. A similarly impressive event is recorded in the Εὐεργετινός. In the desert of Nikopolis there lived a monk. He was looked after by a layman. One day the layman found the monk dead, torn to pieces by a hyena. He prayed to God to learn why this had happened. Through an angel, God answered him: *"This anchorite, being a man, also fell into a slight error, which is why the Lord allowed him to be punished here, by a tragic death, so that in the next life he would be entirely pure in the face of God"* *(Εὐεργετινός, vol. IV, p. 560)*.

b. For greater honour.

Saint John Chrysostom says that most of those who shone in virtue suffered a martyr's death: Abel the Righteous, Saint John the Baptist, Saint Stephen the first martyr and so many others. And by a martyr's death they were more greatly honoured by God. They were given greater crowns.

3. Suicides.

The Church does not bury suicides.

Is it ever possible for the Church to do anything which is not to the benefit of Her flock? Is it ever possible for the Church not to desire the salvation of Her members? Of course not. Which is why She Herself has determined that it is not in the interest of those who commit suicide either to be buried or commemorated.

For the same reason, those who sin and persist in sinning in a diabolical manner should not be commemorated by the Church at the appropriate point in the Holy Liturgy *(Complete Works of Symeon of Thessaloniki)*. Which is why the Holy Liturgy is offered *"for those who live in chastity and holiness of life" (Prayer of the Holy Anaphora)*.

So it is that suicides, too, since they die by sin and in sin, are unworthy of prayer within the Church.

And it is, indeed, horrifying that a person, the masterpiece of creation, the king of nature should be buried like an animal. If we feel sorry, does not God also, Who is the Father and Lover of Mankind? Is He not moved? Does He show no mercy to His servant in such extreme humiliation? We find the answer in the following case:

Saint Pachomios once forbade the burial of a monk who lived in indolence. The monk's relatives were outraged. The enlightened Saint Pachomios, however, told them, amongst other things: *"And you, with this honour, as you conceive it, to the dead man, would increase his distress beyond the grave. While I, by ordering insult and disdain for his corpse, am endeavouring to ensure for him a partial de-*

31

fence in the face of the infallible Judge, or a little relief. Which is precisely why I take no care for the body, but for his eternal soul... God, being the source of goodness, seeks opportunities to find chances to pour out and offer to us the riches of his abundant goodwill and to forgive sins, not only in this present life, but also in the future" (Εὐεργετινός, vol. IV, pp. 556-7).

And so, with this disdain, which sees a person buried like a dog, their soul is comforted by the Righteous Judge. And all those drowned at sea, or torn to pieces by wild beasts, all who have been lost in wars far from their loved ones, and without the prayers of the Church, and all those whose fate is unknown, they, too, because of this contempt will be shown mercy and be comforted by the Righteous Judge.

Many of those engaged in the spiritual struggle, holy people and saints, being gifted with divine enlightenment, have "*envied*" this disdain. And have themselves requested not to be buried, but to be despised and thrown out like animals!

Saint John of Sinai praises those monks who asked their abbot that they should not be buried like people, but should be cast to the wild animals or midstream into a river like unreasoning beasts. "*And not infrequently, that lamp of discretion, the Abbot, paid heed and did so, giving orders that they should be buried without any honour or chanting whatsoever*" *(The Ladder, Logos V, 5)*. At the hour of his death, Saint Arsenios told his disciples to tie a rope round his legs and drag him off to the mountains. Another holy monk also requested the monk living with him to take his body, as soon as he had died, and throw it out into the desert to be eaten by the wild animals and birds: because he felt unworthy of being buried. And his fellow-monk did as he was bidden. And then on the third day, the dead man appeared to him and said: "*Brother, I pray that God will show you mercy as you did me. Believe me, God has been very munificent towards me on account of the disdain for my body, which has lain unburied. God told me: 'Behold, for your great humility, I have ordered that you be with Saint Anthony '*" (Εὐεργετινός, vol. IV, pp. 551-562).

Let us return to the Godly-wise words of the Blessed Pachomios: "*God, being the source of goodness, seeks opportunities to find chances to pour out and offer to us the riches of his abundant goodwill and to forgive sins, not only in this present life, but also in the future*".

4. THE DEPARTURE OF THE SOUL

1. What is the soul?

The most comprehensive definition of the soul would be: "*Man's internal functions*". And these are divided into: reason, comprising the intellect and imagination; longing, being every desire; and passion, being violent feelings, rage, hate and suchlike. Before the Fall, reason, longing and passion were all directed towards God. Everywhere and always, the centre was God. After the Fall, the direction changed and they were turned towards Sin. And the earthly struggle of mankind is to bring back and to offer to God the three parts of the soul.

"*And God formed man of the dust from the ground and breathed into his face the breath of life*" (Genesis 2, 7). Amazing! The soul is the breath of God! We have within us something of God. A mystery. Because God is a mystery. A super- power. Because God is All- powerful. We have a treasury of strengths. Astonishing forces. A giant called the soul!

The soul is something from God. And God is charitable and just. There are, therefore, in every soul, the seeds of charity and justice. An old woman gets on a bus. And someone gives her their seat. This does not mean perfection, simply that they are still people, not animals. That they have got a soul. Even the most unjust love justice, irrespective of whether they pursue it themselves or not. And the worst malefactors love good. Because of the seeds of good in their souls.

The soul does not only have such qualities, however, some of which are shared by animals. It has something incomparably superior. It has spiritual qualities. And when it has been cleansed of sin and of the passions, being now pure, it sees far. And sees things which are not only material, but spiritual as well. Saint Anthony the Great, who was experienced in these matters, informs us: "*I believe that when it is cleansed thoroughly and stands in its true nature, it can become clear-sighted and see more, and farther, than the demons, because it has the Lord Who opens its eyes*". The same is said, more analytically, by Abbas Isaak the Syrian *(Logos 67)*. Which is why Saint Anthony saw the soul of the Blessed Ammun ascending to Heaven, even though he was a fortnight's journey away on foot.

So we have within us, then, something magnificent. A giant. But this giant is drugged. It is sleeping. Snoring. We have given it a powerful sedative and it is sunk in deep sleep. Indifference, indolence, inattention and above all sin are powerful drugs for the soul.

2. When the soul leaves.

a. Awareness.

Saint John of Damascus writes: "*at the last breath, as in a scale, the actions of people are tried*" *(P.G. 96, 156)*. Anyone, therefore, who neglects to keep God's commandments, or who does not struggle zealously for spiritual things, cannot bear the terrible distress "*they will feel un-*

bearable pain at the hour of their death" (*Saint Mark the Ascetic*).

We do not now understand this, or we even doubt it. And justifiably. Because we have no experience of death. And yet! Experience of death will come. "*A stitch in time saves nine*". "*People will then really know that this world is false and deceiving*" (*Abbas Isaak the Syrian*). And they repent! Alexander the Great, as he lay dying, requested that he be buried with one hand outside the coffin, in recognition of the fact that he had achieved nothing in this world. He left it with empty hands, taking nothing with him. The same was felt by George M. Pullman, the American plutocrat and inventor of the railway carriage named after him, Brezhniev, Mao-Tse Tung and a host of others.

b. The pain of the soul.

The soul is a guest of the body. It leaves it unwillingly, "*it is parted with violence*" (*Funeral Service*). Since it can no longer stay there, because of the weakness of the body. Why is the soul "*parted with violence*" from the body? Is it not going to Heaven? To God? Ought it not to be pleased about that? The soul loves, feels pain, has attachments. Therefore it loves, is attached to the body in which for so long it was a guest. Like a married couple, the best married couple. "*For the soul has naturally such a tender bond with its own familiar body that it would never willingly leave it*" (*Saint Gregory Palamas*).

And so the hour of the soul's departure from the body is very distressing. It grieves not only because it is bidding farewell to its own place, its home, its own people, its relations. Above all it grieves because it is bidding farewell to its body, which it naturally loves above all else. And that moment is exceedingly terrible for the soul. *"Alas, what a struggle the soul has, parted from the body" (Funeral Service)*. How it suffers! Which is why the hymnographer says *"It is indeed most terrible, the mystery of death, how the soul is parted from the body, from harmony" (Funeral Service)*. The words of the Church are no exaggeration. Not just *"terrible"*, nor *"most terrible"* but *"indeed most terrible"*. Because the soul *"is cloven by God's will"*. That is, *"cut in two"*. It *"comes unstuck from the flesh"*. And since it is sundered, it suffers like women in difficult labour *(Blessed Niketas Stethatos)*. *"How can I explain the pain and distress I suffered until my soul parted from the body! I would compare those pains to being cast alive and naked into a fire, being seared, writhing in pain and gradually being severed until the soul departs from the body. That is how bitter death is, child"* related the soul of the dead Theodora to the monk Gregorios *(Gregorios the Monk, The Mystery of Death, p. 6, Greek text)*.

And since that moment is so painful, the soul needs comfort at that time. Someone at hand to share the pain. Which is why the Lord had mercy on a negligent monk, precisely because at the hour of his death there was no one beside him to weep for him *(Εὐεργετινός, vol. I, p. 189,7)*.

The Lord lived the anguish of death, felt this pain and prayed! But he interrupted his prayer and ran to His disciples. *"And he found them sleeping; and he said to Peter, 'So could you not stay awake with me for one hour?'"(Matthew 26, 40-41)*.

The Church has a special service for the shattering moment of death. *"Yea Master, Lord our God, give ear to me your sinful and unworthy servant at this hour, and release Your servant (Name) from this unbearable pain and this continuing bitter sickness..."* (Small Euchologion, Service for the Departing of the Soul).

c. The strange thing.

Since death is so terrible, cowardice is natural. Which is why Christ, too, was dismayed: *"Christ feared death, but did not tremble, so that the qualities of both natures could be plainly manifest"* (The Ladder, Logos VI, 4). But how was it that the holy martyrs, e.g. the holy First Martyr Stephen and so many other martyrs and saints, as well as even ordinary lay Christians did not show even this natural cowardice in the face of death? Is this not a stumbling-block? God to show fear and people not to?

Since death is so terrible it is the *"Achilles heel"* for the soul of the Christian! The Devil has been biding his time for this moment. *"The snake which slithers along the earth always follows on our heels, that is, it considers how to do us harm at the moment of our death"* (Saint Cassian). He attempts to create confusion, darkness, despair, hopelessness and disbelief, in the soul! *"My God, my God. Why have you forsaken me"* (Mark XV, 34) cried the Lord as He died. And so the Merciful Lord does not forsake His servants at this most difficult time. He does not abandon them to fight alone with the terrors of death nor with the terrible Devil. He sends them His last earthly gift. He enfolds them in His grace so that they should not feel even this natural dismay that Christ felt (Εὐεργετινός, vol. I, case 7).

The Lord, of course, is not bound by that. He often allows His servants to taste this cowardice and the fear of death for their own good. For forgiveness of their offences and for greater glory. Saint Gregory the Dialogist tells us: "*It occurs that when the souls of the just are to be separated from their bodies, that they fear death exceedingly and become dismayed. In particular, they told me this about a certain man. No sooner had the hour of his death come upon him when he began to fear and be greatly dismayed. After his death, however, he appeared to his disciples in a pure white robe and showed them the glory in which he was. From this we can conclude that the fear of death, and the anguish generated in the soul by this, erased the slight offences which, as a person, he was likely to have committed*" (Εὐεργετινός, vol. III, p. 237, 12).

And so if one sees mortal remains, with anguish, dismay, and confusion engraved on the face, one ought not to conclude that the departed person was a sinner. Simply, they fought with death! There took place what the psalmist describes: "*My heart is in anguish within me, the terrors of death have fallen upon me, Fear and trembling have come upon me and darkness covered me*" (Psalm 54, 5-6).

d. Demons.

It is not only the pain of the soul which makes death terrible. There is something else, just as terrifying! The sight of the demons. The demons rush at the soul to seize it. And the sight of demons is horrible! Much more so when they rush at your soul to seize it. Which is why the Church prays continuously:

"*And now, Lord, may Your hand cover me and Your mercy descend upon me, for my soul is trembling and is greatly pained at its departure from this miserable and de-*

filed body. May it not encounter the evil counsellors of the adversary and be hindered by my sins committed in this world in knowledge or in ignorance. Be gracious to me, Master, and may my soul not behold the gloomy and dark sight of the evil demonsz" (Saturday Midnight Office). And in the Service of Compline "And at the hour of death care diligently for my wretched soul, driving far from it the dark forms of evil spirits".

In the Εὐεργετινός, (vol. I, pp. 125-8), three devastating events are described, which show demons rushing in a mad rage to snatch the soul just at the moment of its departure from the body.

And that moment is vital for the soul. It needs our help. It cries out for help. What help? Prayer! Because the Lord said: "This kind does not depart save by prayer and fasting" (Mark 9, 29). And by our prayer, we can save a soul! The monk Kosmas confessed to his brethren at the time of his death "For I do not know, if I am deserted by you, whether I shall be overcome by them (the demons)" (Menaion for October, synaxarion V of the month, on which day we commemorate the terrible and beneficial vision of Kosmas the Monk). "This serpent cannot swallow me up entirely because of your presence", said one negligent servant of God to the monks who were praying for him at the moment of the departure of his soul from the body. And the result: "My brothers, give thanks to God, because the serpent which had seized me to tear me to pieces fled at your prayers and could not remain here" (Εὐεργετινός, vol. I, p. 126).

God is the same. Unchanging. Merciful. His character does not alter. These things did not happen only then, they happen today, too. To as many as call upon Him. A Mr

G.K. related the following recently: "*On 17/8/1986, at 2 a.m., my mother died. She was an old woman and had had a stroke. Before she breathed her last she started trembling all over, like a fish out of water. We couldn't restrain her. We resorted to prayer. We said the Paraklesis to the Mother of God. As soon as the Paraklesis started, she calmed down. She opened her mouth three times and gave up her soul calmly*".

5. OFFICE AT THE SOUL'S DEPARTING

1. The Preparation.

We still retain the good custom of washing the body of those who have died, and decking them out as if they were going on an official journey.

But this washing of the dead is carried out with particular order, the sign of the Cross being made over them. They are then anointed with oil either from the lamp in the altar or with that from the Sacrament of the Anointing Service, which in older days was performed especially for the dead person. *"For this reason, then, they dip a sponge in water and make the sign of the cross on the forehead, the eyes, the mouth and the breast, and again on the knees and the hands and they then anoint the dead person so that the oil signifies that used in former times by athletes, implying that the departed one has struggled well and in the fear of God and wants to be worthy of the Compassion of God and of the bright joy of the Divine Light"* ("Άπαντα" *Saint Symeon of Thessaloniki, p.309*).

Thereafter, they are dressed in new clothes. *"A new shroud; a new mantle of incorruption which they are to take"* (*Saint John Chrysostom*). A priest, however, when he departs is attired in all his priestly garments, according to the practice of the Church. His right hand blesses, he holds the Gospel to his breast, while his face is covered by the *"Air"*, the same cloth that covers the Body of the Lord, as if the Church were saying that the face of the priest has as much holiness as the Divine Liturgy. Relatives wear black, mourning. In Alexandria, in Skete, the monks did not wear black at the passing away of one of their brothers, but white. As a sign of the victory of the departed brother over the three enemies: the world, the flesh and the devil.

When the Most Holy Mother of God was departing this life, the Apostles were scattered throughout the inhabited world. And yet a cloud miraculously brought them to Jerusalem to the Mother of God's house. The Mother of the Teacher of the Holy Apostles fell asleep and the friends and acquaintances of the Lord were required to be present at her funeral. That teaches us that it is an obligation, a duty of Christians, when our brethren leave this world, to follow the dead from the house to the church and from the church to the grave, giving them a last embrace and entreating God to forgive their sins.

2. The Procession.

The Church honours the dead person, as does the public by its attendance in large numbers. Burial is an honour for the dead. The greatest honour in this world. When else such a crowd? When else such honour from the Church? When a person is baptised, the priest awaits them in the church. The same when they get married. But when they are buried, the priest does not wait for them to be brought to the church, but goes to their home. And they come to church together. And with incense. With sacramental fans. With candles, while on the way the hymn of the angels is chanted: *"Holy God, Holy Mighty, Holy Immortal have mercy upon us"*, just as happens on Great Friday when the Winding-Sheet is carried in procession round the streets! *"We escort the departed with psalms and hymns, manifesting the thanks we give to Christ for their death... Chrism, olive oil, aid on the road hence, incense and candles; 'freed from the darkness they have gone to the true light' "* (Saint John Chrysostom).

3. In the Church.

The dead person now lies in the middle of the church, and the funeral service is chanted. The focus of the service is the vanity of life and the fervent supplication of the Church, towards the Merciful God, that He will forgive the sins of the departed. The congregation gazes at the dead person. With the flight of the soul from the body, the latter is paralysed, it returns to its original form, automatically becoming clay. *"For the spirit has deserted its tabernacle. Its clay has grown black, the vessel is shattered, voiceless, senseless, dead and immobile"*. Here is another verse: *"The eyes have turned inward, the feet are bound, the hands are at rest and the hearing, too, the tongue is imprisoned in silence, committed to the tomb"* (Funeral Service).

"The verdant meadow is fit for sheep. And the teaching and remembrance of death is the most fitting for every logical sheep, and has the power to cure all manner of sores" (The Ladder, Logos to Pimen, 81). If the mere recollection of death is so beneficial, how much more so must gazing upon it be! However tough a person is, an earthquake, great or small, occurs within them and the mountainous ice-bergs

of indifference are reduced or even melted. Let them have read all the books in the world, a veritable ocean, one drop will have remained within them. At that moment, however, the drop is an ocean for the soul. Everyone boasts of their future. Their end. Their career. Here they *"freeze"*. Their wings are clipped. Here is their life. Here are their joys. Here are their diversions.

4. At the grave.

The body of the departed person is laid in the grave, facing east, awaiting the Lord Who will return thence *"to judge both the living and the dead"*. *"When the mortal remains have been laid in the grave, oil is poured over them in the form of the Cross, as was handed down by the Apostles, and Dionysios writes that at burial the dead are to be anointed. As at baptism there are oil and water, so at the end these should be brought to those who have lived in faith and piety in the same way, as a type of these...when everyone has made twelve prostration to God for the expiation of the departed... each one leaves, deep in meditation and concern, and contemplating the fact that the same is going to happen to them+. ("Άπαντα", Saint Symeon of Thessaloniki, p. 309).*

5. The Honour to the Body.

A corpse is no longer a person, but is death. What is buried, therefore, is not such and such a person, but their death, their dead body. Corpse, dead material, wood, stone it is all the same!

The Church honours the body, however, as if it were a living person! It censes it, we embrace it. Precisely because it was a co-agent in virtue.

6. The official procession.

"Now the rich man died and was buried" (Luke XVI, 23). Since he died, it is obvious that he would be buried. But why does the Holy Gospel report *"and he was buried"*. He was rich, and as a rich man he was buried. With honour and glory. A magnificent funeral. But this was harmful for his soul. If he did any good in life, he now enjoyed his recompense with a magnificent funeral. Had he been given a humble burial, he would not have lost his reward! He would, indeed, have had a double reward. First for the good he had done and secondly for the humiliation of his body! *"Listen carefully. That impious man had performed one small good act in his life and the Lord allowed him to enjoy it here with this splendid and imposing funeral, so that he shall not find any rest at all in the next life"*, explained an angel of the Lord to a layman who was scandalized by the magnificent funeral of an impious rich man (*Εὐεργετινός, vol. IV, p. 560*). Which is why monks are buried very simply, poorly, humbly, with their cowls over their faces. Their mortal remains are not put into a coffin, while their graves are very simple, with just a wooden cross. It is worth noting here the following remarkable piece of information. The corpse of a monk does not suffer rigor mortis nor does it become cold. It remains warm and supple as it was in life. And this is of symbolic importance. Monasticism as an ascetic struggle, is the passing from corruptibility to incorruptibility, from death to immortality. And *"as a sign"* of this, the Lord preserves the corpses of monks as if they were alive.

7. Weeping.

Parting is a trial. The Christians of Ephesus mourned inconsolably when they were separated from the Apostle Paul. *"And they all wept and embraced Paul and kissed him, sorrowing most of all because of the word he had spoken, that they should see his face no more" (Acts XX, 37-8).*

The Apostle Paul wrote to the Christians of Thessaloniki, how he missed them and wanted very much to see them. *"But since we were bereft of you, brethren, for a short time, in person not in heart, we endeavoured the more eagerly and with great desire to see you face to face" (I Thessalonians II, 17).* And to console himself and the Thessalonians, he sent the Apostle Timothy. *(I Thessalonians III, 2)*

Saint Paul himself went to preach in Troas and did not do so, because he did not find the Apostle Titus there. He was saddened. *"Sorrow of the heart saps one's strength" (Wisdom of Sirach 38, 18).* He was not in the mood to preach! Who? He who had suffered everything for the sake of his Christ. And he left for Macedonia. *"When I came to Troas to preach the gospel of Christ, a door was opened for me in the Lord; but my mind could not rest because I did not find my brother Titus there. So I took leave of them and went on to Macedonia" (II Corinthians II, 12-13).* No-one can avoid the pain of parting, then, however saintly they are!

And if temporary parting costs us so much, how much more so the permanent separation which comes with death! Which is why sorrow and pain are inevitable. They are the *"undeniable passions"*. And where there are sadness, pain and sighing, then weeping follows.

From a psychological point of view, weeping is necessary. The sadness is lifted. It is transformed into tears. It leaves the person, who then finds relief. So the best comfort for those who are in pain, in sorrow or in bereavement is to be left to weep. They get it off their chests. When they are prevented, they suffer psychological damage. They break down. Sorrow builds up inside them and breeds numerous dangers. If a mother does not cry when she loses her child, when will she cry? If a man does not cry when he loses his brother, when will he cry?

Granted. But we are Christians. It does not do for us to cry! We often hear that. Quite right. We are Christians, but we are people, too! Not stones. The ancient Greeks used to say that inanimate objects and beasts do not cry. *"My child, let your tears fall for the dead, and as one who is suffering grievously begin the lament...Let your weeping be bitter and your wailing fervent; observe the mourning according to his merit, for one day, or two, to avoid criticism; then be comforted in your sorrow"* (Wisdom of Sirach 38, 16-17). And Christ Himself wept, seeing the rest of the Jews and Mary, the dead man's sister, bewailing the loss of Lazarus: *"When Jesus saw her weeping, and the Jews who came with her also weeping, he was deeply moved in spirit and troubled"* (John XI, 33). Going to the tomb of Lazarus, he wept again: *"Then Jesus, deeply moved again, came to the tomb"* (ibid., 38).

The hymnology of the Church presents the Most Holy Mother of God as mourning the death of the Lord: *"Do not lament over me, Mother, beholding in the tomb"* (Great Saturday Matins, ode 9). The great Hierarch of our Church, Saint Basil, mourned the death of his beloved mother. This is what he himself wrote: *"Now through my sins I have lost her, too, the only comfort that I had in this life. And do not laugh at me for lamenting at being left an orphan at this age, but forgive me for not having the strength to bear easily being parted from a soul the like of which I do not see among those who remain here"* (Letter to Eusebios of Samosata). And again, when he heard of the death of a child, he cried and wept *(Letter 5)*.

The Funeral Service does not prevent a Christian from crying. On the contrary, it justifies it entirely. *"What separation, brethren, what mourning at the present critical moment!"* And again: *"Beholding me laid out without voice or breath, all of you weep for me, brothers and friends, relations and acquaintances"* [3]. All of which suffices for us to be able to say that tears are not a proof of disbelief, but are simply something human, which is why the Church countenances them. Since it is impossible for people not to grieve.

One clarification.

We should weep. But like Christ did before Lazarus. Like the Mother of God before the dead Christ. Like the Apostle Paul. Like Basil the Great, like all the saints. That is, without railing against God, because that is a mortal sin. We should weep in the belief that our brother or sister has passed on from earth to Heaven. Not *"like those without hope"* (I Thessalonians IV, 14). *"We do not abjure grief but counsel that which is good rather than that which arises from*

3. It is not by chance that the hymnographer puts these words into the mouth of the dead person. The tears of the relatives are a consolation for the soul of the departed. (Εὐεργετινός, vol. I, p. 189, 7).

despair" *(Saint Gregory of Nyssa, PG, vol. 46, 537).*

Death as parting is a stabwound for the soul. *"And a sword will pierce your own soul, too," (Luke II, 35),* prophesied Symeon the Just, meaning the death of Christ on the Cross, which was painful for the Mother of God. And whoever bears this wound, this trial without complaint is crowned a martyr! *"If your were cut up into pieces and you bore it bravely and glorified God, you would have great reward. The same is true now, when you are suffering pain in your soul" (Saint John Chrysostom).*

6. THE BURIAL

1. Where?

From the earliest years of Christianity, the custom obtained of burying the faithful even within the church, either in special places or just in front of the Royal Doors. Which is why Saint Ephraim the Syrian made provision in his will not to be buried in church, nor under the altar of the church. This was also the practice in Greece, especially in the islands, until recently, until the years of slavery under the Turks. Today, however, the sole place where the dead are buried is the special cemetery.

When the body enters the earth, it begins to decompose in the grave. It corrupts, it becomes one with the earth: *"Dust thou art, to dust returneth"*. It is said that the first part to decompose is the eye, because through it, the sight of the fruit, sin came into the world. And since the body corrupts, it inevitably smells.

Where the dead are buried is a matter of importance, however. Tobit said to his child: *"My child, when I die, bury me, and do not neglect your mother... When she dies, bury her beside me in the same grave"* (Tobit IV, 3-5). It was a punishment for the prophet Achia not to be buried in the land of his fathers *(I Kings XIII, 22)*. When Moses left

Egypt, he took with him the bones of Joseph, fulfilling the desire of the latter *(Genesis 50, 25)*. It was Jacob's desire to be buried in Canaan, although he died in Egypt: *"My father made me swear saying, 'I am about to die: in my tomb which I hewed out in the land of Canaan, there shall you bury me'" (Genesis 50, 5)*. Saint Andronikos wanted to die where his wife, Saint Athanasia was buried. The first Archbishop of Serbia, Saint Savvas (+1235) took the bones of his father, Saint Symeon, from the Holy Mountain to Serbia, to the Monastery of Studenica. Saint John Chrysostom, buried in exile in Komana in Asia Minor, consistently refused in a miraculous way, to have his relics transferred to Constantinople. Constantine the Great's general, Leontius, fell seriously ill. He was made well again by Saint Demetrios, once he had reverenced the saint's tomb. On his return to his homeland, he asked for relics from the saint, in order to build a church there in his memory. The saint appeared to him, however, and told him: *"Do not break me up, but rather leave me whole in my own land" (Μέγας Συναξαριστής, October, p. 602)*. The modern saint Arsenios of Cappadocia said to a certain servant of the Lord *"You get off here. I'm getting off at Thessaloniki, because I live near there" (Saint Arsenios of Cappadocia, p. 44 [English translation])*. The servant of God Eleftheria, buried in a Turkish graveyard, appears to have found no rest for her soul *(ibid. p. 135)*. It seems that the Most Holy Mother of God also had a preference: *"Bury my body in the village of Gethsemane"*. All this, then, shows that souls find rest when they are buried where they want to be.

2. Disinterment-Undecomposed corpses.

In about three years, the dead body decomposes. There are, of course, also cases where even after three years, the body has not decomposed. This may be due to the morphology of the ground or to the particular features of the corpse. In natural circumstances, the body ought to have decomposed within 5-7 years. And once it has decomposed, it is disinterred. The bones are taken and washed in wine and placed in a special box. They are then brought to church, to the centre and a normal Remembrance Service is held. They are then placed in a special little church house or put back in the grave. If, however, the corpse has not decomposed, and is, moreover, disfigured, swollen up like a drum, then this is worrying. It is a sign that the soul is being tortured. It is suffering. Because it is *"bound"* to something. So what is happening?

a. It may have been cursed by someone[4].

b. The person concerned may have cursed, anathematised or sworn by his or her own person.

c. They may have been very unjust (stolen, done

---

4. It is uncertain whether a layman's curse will *"take"*. That of a clergyman, however, is sure to, because the clergyman is a priest. And being a priest means power. And a curse is the use of power. We have innumerable and devastating cases which show the astonishing action of a curse laid by clergy! Even if the person involved becomes a saint and a martyr, if he is bound by a curse of the clergy, this bond is not loosed unless the special prayer of forgiveness is read. A relevant case is cited in the Menologion for October 15.

wrong).

The Church has adopted special prayers of forgiveness *"for every curse and excommunication on the departed, to be read by a bishop, or, failing that, a Spiritual Father where there is no bishop present"*. And amongst other things, the prayers say: *"whether this your servant (Name) has fallen under the curse of father or mother or has anathematised himself or has embittered exceedingly one of the clergy and been bound by him with unloosable bonds or has fallen under the most heavy excommunication of a bishop and through indolence or laziness has not sought forgiveness, forgive them now through me, the sinner"*.

In the Life of Saint Dionysios, Archbishop of Zakynthos, we read: *" It happened that when the saint was in the town, they opened a tomb in the Church of Saint Nicholas of the Strangers, so called because strangers were buried there. It is also the Cathedral of Zakynthos. In this tomb they were going to bury the mortal remains of someone else, and found there the corpse of a woman who had died some time before, which was complete, with all its clothes, because she had died either under the bond of excommunication or in a state of tribulation. And so her relatives came and fell down at the feet of the saint, begging him with tears to go to this church to read the prayer of forgiveness for this corpse which was under a curse, in the hope that the Lord would pay heed to his prayer. The saint was moved to pity by their tears and went to the church in the dead of night, taking with him his deacon and the vicar of the church. When he saw the corpse, he told them to take it out of the tomb and to stand it upright in one of the prayer-stalls of the church. He then put on his vestments, and knelt and prayed for a good long time, beg-*

56

ging God with fervent tears to free this undecomposed body from the bond of excommunication. When the saint read over her the prayer of forgiveness - what a miracle! - this lifeless corpse, as if it were animate, inclined its head towards the saint, as if in gratitude for the great grace which it had received, and fell to the earth and decomposed completely into dust and bones...He performed a similar miracle for the excommunicated corpse of another man in the village of Kastarion" (Μέγας Συναξαριστής, December, p. 491).

7. THE TOLL-HOUSES

1. Sinners.

Sin is a stench[5], which drives our guardian angels away! We continuously entreat them *"do not desert me because of my incontinence"* . So anyone who lives all the time in sin, has already driven away his or her guardian angel, and become a servant of demons. At their death, the demons come and take their souls and take them straight to Hell, *"Fool, this night they shall require your soul of you"*, i.e. the demons *(Luke XII, 21)*. Because *"stained and unrepentant souls are received by the demons" (Saint Theodoros, Bishop of Edessa)*.

Because they are such sinners, they will not stand

5. On the other hand, virtue is a fragrance, an aroma for our guardian angel, which draws the angel closer to us. Fasting, for example, queen of the virtues because it cleanses the soul of the stench of sin and evil, gives joy to our guardian angels, and because of this joy they sacrifice all the more for us. *"For the wanton insults of the demons do not discourage the faster, but the guardians of your life, the Angels, will all the more diligently stand beside you who are cleansed by the fast" (Aposticha of the Praises, Monday of Cheese-week).*

before Christ, as that is an honour! *"Therefore the wicked will not stand in the judgement"* (Psalm 1, 5). Which is why, in the Gospel which is read on Meatfare Sunday *(Matthew 25, 31-46)*, He does not judge the greedy, the murderers, deceivers, adulterers and libertines! Not that the world does not have sinner. But precisely because they are unworthy of such an honour! They will be resurrected, not to be judged, but for greater condemnation *(Saint Gregory Palamas, homily XIII, 10)*.

2. The Righteous.

The righteous person *"does not come into judgement"* (John V, 24). They go straight to Paradise, without passing through the toll-houses *"(The soul) passes through the air without hindrance, without being troubled in the least by the evil spirits"* (Blessed Theognostos). And that is the hope and prayer of our Church: *"may my soul not see the gloomy and dark sight of the evil spirits, but may your bright and humble Angels receive it"* (Saturday Midnight Office).

It is not only angels who receive the souls of the just, but the Most Holy Mother of God herself and even Christ Himself! Christ Himself came and received the soul of the Mother of God. *"And you my Son and God receive my spirit"*. When Saint Sisoes breathed his last, Anthony the Great, the Holy Apostles, the Angels and Christ Himself came, saying *"bring me the vessel of the desert"*. It is clear, therefore, that the Most Holy Mother of God, Saint Sisoes and so many other saints and martyrs went straight to Heaven. Bypassing the toll-houses.

Therefore the toll-houses are for those who leave this world in a luke-warm, torpid moral state. They are for those whose flight from this world takes place in the winter of passions or on a sabbath *(Matthew 24, 20)* (i.e. without having cultivated the virtues). They are *"answerable to be judged and examined in the time of retribution" (Blessed Theognostos)*. *"When the Teacher spoke of flight on the Sabbath and in the winter, He foretold darkly, as in a riddle, the storm of the present age, which is the seventh day of the week, when the end shall return as the winter" (Triodion, Great Monday evening, Compline, ode 8).*

3. What are the toll-houses?

Much has been written about the toll-houses, but the clearest and most comprehensive description is that given by an angel of the Lord to Saint Makarios of Egypt. We quote the relevant passage: *"from the earth to heaven there is a ladder, and each rung has a cohort of demons. These are called toll-houses and the evil sprits meet the soul and bring its handwritten accounts and show these to the angels, saying: on this day and on such and such of the month this soul did that: either it stole or fornicated or committed adultery or was effeminate or lied or encouraged someone to an evil deed. And everything else evil which it has done, they show to the angels.*

The angels then show whatever good the soul has done, charity or prayer or liturgies or fasting or anything else. And the Angels and the demons reckon up, and if they find the good greater than the evil, the angels sieze the soul and take it up to the next rung, while the demons gnash their teeth like wild dogs and make haste to snatch that pitiable soul from the hands of the Angels. The soul, meanwhile, cowers, and terror encompasses it and it makes as if to hide in the bosom of the Angels and there is a great discussion and much turmoil until that soul is delivered from the hands of those demons.

And they come again to another rung and there find another toll-house, fiercer and more horrible. And in this, too, there is much uproar and great and indescribable turbulence as to who shall take that wretched soul. And shouting out aloud, the demons examine the soul, causing terror and saying: "Where are you going? Aren't you the one who fornicated and thoroughly polluted Holy Baptism? Aren't you the one who polluted the angelic habit? Get back. Get down. Get yourself to dark Hell. Get yourself to the outer fire. Get going to the worm that never sleeps".

Then if it be that that soul is condemned, the evil demons bear it off to below the earth, to a dark and distressing spot. And woe to that soul in which that person was born. And who shall tell, Holy Father, that straits in which the condemned souls will find themselves in this place! But if the soul is found clean and sinless, it goes up to Heaven with such joy".

It has been observed that those possessed by demons are able to tell some people their sins, referring in detail to the time and place when they were committed. But they only disclose unconfessed sins. Confessed sins, for the demons, are not sins. *"Blessed are they whose transgressions have been forgiven, whose sins have been revealed"* (Psalm 31, 1). And this comes about through the soul saving sacrament of Holy Confession. The same is true for the toll-houses, the aerial demons. They check only unconfessed sins. Confessed sins, whatever and however so many they be are forgotten by the evil spirits! ... *"and so ascending again*

I asked the angels, saying: in what way can a person's sins be forgiven in the world and be expunged from the books of the aerial demons? And they answered me: "These can always be erased and forgiven when someone repents and confesses their sins".

4. What should we do?

The toll-houses, then, are a terrifying ordeal for the soul. Fear, terror and anguish take over the soul. *"Then they would have swallowed us up alive, when their anger was kindled against us; then the flood would have swept us away, the torrent would have gone over us; then over us would have gone the raging waters" (Psalm 123, 3-5).* In these critical moments, the soul needs help from us. The Lord said: *"This kind will not depart save by prayer and fasting" (Matthew 17, 21).* The soul, then, needs prayer from us. The demons pleaded with the Lord *"not to command them to depart into the abyss" (Luke 8, 31),* but to allow them to go into the swine, *"to allow them to enter these" (ibid.).* And the Lord heard the demons' plea! Whose? The demons', who are continuously doing battle with the Lord! *"And he gave them leave" (ibid. verse 32).* Will not the Lord, then, attend to a similar plea from Christians, who struggle to carry out His will? Of course He will! Much more so! *(Saint John of Karpathos).* Which is why we should pray fervently to God the Merciful. And why we keep a wake for the dead person.

Saint Seraphim of Sarov relates: *"Two nuns passed on. Both had been abbesses. The Lord revealed to me that their souls were having difficulty getting through the aerial toll-houses. Three days and nights, I, a lowly sinner, prayed and begged the Mother of God for their salvation. The good-*

63

ness of the Lord, through the prayers of the Most Holy Mother of God, finally had mercy upon them. They passed the aerial toll-houses and received forgiveness of sins" (Life of Saint Seraphim). It is of significance here that the Lord revealed to Saint Seraphim that these souls were in difficulty at the toll-houses. Why did the Lord disclose this? So that the saint would pray. And why to the saint? Because he was a saint. And his prayer was made with boldness. Which is why it was heard.

And the candles which we light next to the corpse, what is their significance? They are prayer. Even the arms of the dead person are not left down by the side, but are placed in the form of the cross, so that the dead body, with the form of the cross, can give support to the soul.

The most effective weapon of all, however, against the terrible aerial demons is Holy Communion. It is the fire which drives them away! In this way, the soul passes through the toll-houses painlessly, together with the holy angels. Saint John Chrysostom says: "And someone else told me, who had not been told it by anyone else but had been deemed worthy to see and hear it himself, that those who are about to leave this place, if they take communion with a clear conscience, are received and surrounded by angels when their souls depart, because of Holy Communion" (Talks on the Priesthood, VI, 24). Which is why the Church, through a canon, ordains Holy Communion for those at the point of death (Canon XIII, Ist Ecumenical Synod).

5. Reception of the souls.

" Just so, I tell you, there is joy before the angels of God over one sinner who repents" (Luke XV, 10). And this is clear from the parable of the Prodigal Son *(Luke XV, 11-32)*.

Now if the angels rejoice at the repentance of a sinner (whose salvation is not assured, because people vacillate), how much more do they do so when servants of God leave this world as victors! And their salvation is certain! Then, indeed, there is great celebration in Heaven.

Saint John Chrysostom says:

"A king is at war, fighting a dangerous enemy. And he defeats him, routs him, destroys him. He returns to his city as victor. How do people receive him? With acclamation for his great triumph. This is precisely the way in which Heaven receives the souls which fought on earth against the Ruler of the World in this age. And defeated him. And now return to Heaven as victors! 'Open wide the gates and receive above the world the Mother of the everlasting light' " (Vespers, Dormition of the Mother of God). And the angel of the Lord said to Saint Makarios: *"If a soul be found that is pure and sinless, it ascends with lights and incense and they embrace it"*.

It is not only the angels who rejoice and receive the soul, but the saints, the righteous and the relatives, too. *"While the Angel was telling me this, I suddenly heard a great noise, because Angels were arriving bearing a soul, chanting psalms, with incense and candles shedding illumination, and they accompanied it with an endless train of candles, and it came also with great joy and boldness, while the souls of the righteous arrived to meet it"* (Terrible and profitable vision, Μέγας Συναξαριστής, August, p. 112).

The strange thing is that in America, people who are utterly worldly, and clinically dead, have had their souls leave them for a short time and go to the next world. They saw the toll-houses and the reception of their souls by their friends and relatives. And, on coming round, they told all this to people who were indifferent; unbelievers, and scientists, who were set thinking deeply by it! The *"escorting"* of the souls.

When the soul has passed the dreadful toll-houses, it rejoices. It exults. Then it prostrates itself before the Creator *(Blessed Theognostos)*. *"Then it comes to the Lord's throne and prostrates itself before Our Lord and God Jesus Christ"* *(Revelation of the Angel etc)*. Then it is *"escorted"*. We read in the revelation of the angel: *"Then it sees the ranks of the Holy Apostles, the Holy Martyrs, the Holy Fathers, the nine cohorts of Holy Angels, that unspeakable brilliance, and hears that angelic melody and irresistible beauty.*

After its obeisance, the Angels then return it to the earth and point out to it those places in which it dwelt in this life and weigh up its deeds, both good and evil, saying: "Here you slandered, there you behaved foolishly, here you murdered, there you perjured, here you were unjust, there you blasphemed, here you lent money at interest, there you were drunk, here you were contentious, there offensive." And then again the good: "Here you gave charity, there you fasted, here you repented, there you attended the liturgy; here again the liturgy, here a service of intercession; there vigils, here prayer; there prayer on bended knee, here upright; there continence" and so on, continuing until the ninth day. And on the ninth day, it again ascends to prostrate itself, as on the third.

After the second obeisance, the Angels again bear it into the world, showing it Paradise, the bosom of Abraham, the tabernacles and the halls where the righteous repose.

They show it also the torments of the sinners...Having seen all this, it is then brought back to make an obeisance on the fortieth day, which is why Memorial Services are held for the dead, since the soul is due on the fortieth day to be told the decision and go where the Merciful Lord has appointed, according to the works and practices which it performed in the world. And it settles in the place ordered by the Lord until the day of the resurrection, when the body will also arise and enjoy the reward of its works".

8. SOULS AND THE WORLD

1. Communication.

"The soul which leaves a person has: sight, hearing, speech, memory, feelings and a few other qualities which it had while in the body". This is what an angel told a newly-baptised Serb, Dushan. These are the characteristics of the soul. And where the soul is, there, too, are its characteristics. Therefore, the soul hears and remembers and feels. But how? In its own way! We cannot understand that. However hard we try. Because now our souls are in our bodies. In any case, sight, hearing and so on are not due exclusively to eyes and ears. After all a corpse has eyes but does not see. And ears, but does not hear. It follows that something else makes it see and hear: the soul. And this soul, which makes the eyes see and the ears hear, can see and hear by itself.

The Apostle Peter, enlightened by the Holy Spirit, knew that after his death there would be remembrance of and communication with this earthly world. Which is why he writes: *"And I shall see to it that after my departure you may be able at any time to recall these things"* (2 Peter I, 15).

2. Those in Hell.

Do they remember us?

"Then I beg you, father, to send him to my father's house, for I have five brothers, so that he may warn them, lest they also come to this place of torment" (Luke XVI, 27) Words of the Lord Himself and therefore beyond question. The rich man in Hell, then, remembers his father's house and his five brothers. And, most importantly, he is interested in them. Not in what they will eat or drink, but in their salvation *"On that day all their plans perish"* (Psalm 145, 4), that is worldly considerations of the flesh. The idolatrous priest, who was in Hell, recognised Saint Makarios of Egypt who was praying on earth for the damned. And they were comforted. *"And you're Makarios who have the Holy Spirit within you"*.

A certain God-fearing person confessed the following: he had a brother, a wastrel and a blasphemer. He died and went to Hell. One day the surviving, God-fearing brother fell into ecstasy. An Angel of the Lord led him through terrible, wild places to see his brother. They went up to the top of a mountain. He looked down and saw smoke and fire and heard voices groaning! And he heard the voice of his brother moaning and saying: *"Brother, save me!"*.

There are innumerable such instances. But these suffice to convince us that those in Hell remember the world. And cry for help!...

3. The Righteous.

Do they remember us?

"And they cried out in a loud voice, "Sovereign Lord, Holy and True, will you not judge and avenge our blood on those who inhabit the earth?" (Revelation VI, 10). It seems from this that the righteous see and follow what is happening in the world: whom God punishes and whom not. Which is why they "are disappointed" with God because He delays and does not punish sinners. And this is the faith of our Holy Fathers: "And we have remained here observing the commandments of the Lord and keeping the ordinances of the fathers, believing that even after their removal to the Lord they have stayed with us and attend to all our requests" (Abbas John Celix, Εὐεργετινός, vol I, p. 471).

Saint Nektarios told the sisters of his monastery: "When I die, do not fear. From above, too, where I shall be, I shall be watching over you. And I shall protect you".

After his death, two nuns were quarrelling over a brush. The saint appeared to a virtuous Christian and told him: "Come to my house and bring a brush"!

In the Life of Saint John of Sinai we read: "Now when our new Moses, our most blessed Abbot John, was about to depart to the Lord, his brother, Abbas George, was at his side, crying. He said to him: "So you're leaving me and going? I was praying that you would send me on in front". Then Abbas John answered: "Do not be sad and do not worry. Because if I find boldness before the Lord, I shall not leave you behind me for as much as a year". And this is what happened. Within ten months George departed likewise to go to the Lord (The Ladder). What is important here is that

Saint John did not forget his word, the promise he had given to his brother What he had said on earth, he remembered in Heaven!

Exactly the same thing happened with the monk Isidoros. *"If I find boldness before the Lord, I shall soon have you with me, so that we shall be inseparable there, too"*, he had said to the door-keeper of the monastery. *"And seven days after he fell asleep, he took to his side the door-keeper of the Monastery, too"* (The Ladder, Logos XXI).

Other cases:

A monk begged a gardener to throw him, naked out onto the mountain, as soon as he died. The gardener complied. Three days after his death, he appeared to the gardener and thanked him, because he had found mercy with God (*Εὐεργετινός, vol. IV p. 562*). He did not forget the gardener, nor the good he had done him. And he felt obliged to thank him!

The following is also related: In the area around Nafpaktos, a man and his wife, Konstantinos and Paraskevi, did not always live in harmony. The wife, Paraskevi, died. At which she appeared to her husband and said to him: *"We haven't forgiven one another! Go to my grave and say three times "Paraskevi, I forgive you!"* The dead Paraskevi remembered the grumbling, her husband, and forgiveness. The amazing thing in this case, is that The Rudder directs: *"That when there is enmity between two people and one of them dies, the survivor must go to the grave of the deceased and ask forgiveness, as if the other were alive..."* (The Rudder, Greek text p. 716, Note 2,c).

To continue:

Six years ago, a virtuous priest from Agrinio appeared

to his spiritual son, who was about to have an operation for a serious illness at the *"Evangelismos"* hospital in Athens. He cheered him up and assured him that he would get well. Which is what happened. And the following event also took place: at the time of his appearance in the hospital in Athens, the earth over his grave in Agrinio was heaving! The soul of the virtuous priest was watching over his spiritual son. And suffering with him. And he interceded with God. *"Alexandra is suffering with you in your illness and wants you to be healed"*, said Saint Seraphim of Sarov to a woman who was desperately ill and to whom the dead Alexandra, the first abbess of the Monastery of Diveyevo, appeared.

Here, too, the events related are innumerable and intensely moving. We have selected these merely as examples. And what is true for those souls, is true also for all others. That is, they remember us, watch over us, take an interest in us, want what is good for us, suffer with us. And how? Can they take an interest in everything? Can they remember so much and so many? The soul of itself has great power. Even here on earth, when it is in the body, how many people do we know? And we increase the number of our acquaintances all the time. And how many do we remember? But when it leaves the body, freed, and at the same time united with God, then its power becomes inconceivable!

Only God, however, is everywhere present. Not the angels, not the saints, not even the Most Holy Mother of God. The souls are not, therefore, turned towards us all the time. They are also with us. When and for how long, we do not know.

4. They hymn God in church.

The righteous are divided into groups and descend at night to earth, to churches, where they glorify God together. For information on this, see the Menaion for September 8...a most profitable narrative concerning love. And Saint Arsenios of Cappadocia, pp. 27-8 [English translation].

Elderly, simple, humble Christians relate how, in the older days, spending the night outside the church, they would see lights inside and hear chanting, even though the churches were empty! To the humble and simple, the Lord grants heavenly treasures. *"I shall give you hidden treasures" (Isaiah 45, 3).*

5. They pray for us.

"Blessed is he who has seed in Zion, and his own people in Jerusalem" (Isaiah, 31, 9 [Septuagint version]) "So what, if he is a libertine and if he is a drunkard and idolater, is he blessed because he has descendants in Zion and his own people in Jerusalem?" (Saint John of Damascus). Or again, if his descendants, his own people, are libertines, drunkards and idolaters, is he blessed simply because he has descendants in Zion and his own people in Jerusalem? Assuredly not. But this passage has a spiritual interpretation. Zion, Jerusalem, are Paradise. And blessed is the person who has his or her own relatives in Paradise. Precisely because they pray for them! This is why Saint Arsenios says: *"Do good to your neighbour, so that when they leave this world and go to the Lord they will intercede for you and you will find good" (Εὐεργετινός, vol. I, p. 538).* They entreat

74

God for us, without us asking them to do so. They do it by themselves. Let us remember the brothers who were in Paradise and begged God that their remaining brother, who had sinned on earth, might be killed and his soul saved. Indeed, they pray with greater boldness and greater pain, because now they know better what paradise means! Which is why Revelation says: *"And they cried out in a loud voice saying" (Revelation VI, 10).* Not simply that they prayed, but that they *"cried out in a loud voice".*

6. Can we pray to them?

If one of our loved ones leaves this world full of virtues, a saint, without having been declared such by the Church, can we pray to them? To entreat them for a request of ours? Saint Gregory the Dialogist refers to a monk who prayed fervently to his abbot, who had just died, begging him to take him with him. As, indeed, happened *(Εὐεργετινός, vol. III, p. 216).*

From this we learn that we, too, can ask for the prayers of our God-fearing deceased brethren.

7. What appearance do souls have?

Souls are immaterial. So how do they appear and become visible? Perceptible? By God's condescension! God allows the soul to take on a certain form, to become visible, since otherwise it would not be. We, who are material, cannot see the soul, which is immaterial. But this form that it takes is not actually the soul itself.

Because its body is in the ground, how does it appear in corporeal form? It has simply taken on a certain form in order to become visible to us. The same is true of the angels and saints.

And again, this form may not be the soul of some person dear to us. It may be an angel sent from the Lord. This occurs when the soul is *"not free"*, or is praying or is elsewhere, because the soul is not All-powerful, nor everywhere present. The soul does not appear of its own accord, after all.

The angels do nothing of their own accord. Neither do the souls. When they want, they seek permission from the Lord *(Γεροντικό of the Holy Mountain, vol. II, p. 112)*. Or when they do not ask, they are sent, charged by God Himself! For God is much more loving towards Mankind than the souls of our own people and than all the saints.

9. THE SOULS AMONG THEMSELVES

1. The Just

Do they know each other?

"The glory you have given me, I have given them, that they may one day be one, even as we are one" (John 17, 22). Where there is unity, there is love. And where there is love, there is communion and communication. And, it follows, acquaintance. Paradise means love. And therefore unity, communion, communication and at the same time acquaintance. Saint Symeon the New Theologian says: "If, therefore, the saints become like God and will know God as well as God knows them and if as the Father knows the Son, the Son knows the Father, then the Saints will see and know each other" (Τά Εὑρισκόμενα, p. 230).

Saint Makarios asked the Angel of the Lord: "Tell me, Holy Angel, if the departed know one another in that eternal world?" And the answer came: " Listen, holy father, as in this world people sleep until the morning, and the next day arise and recognise those whom they knew the day before, and greet them and talk to them and often sit together rejoicing and questioning one another, so likewise does it happen in that world; each one knows the other and they rejoice and *talk together"*. Thus, Anthony the Great wanted to meet Saint Pachomios, while he was still alive. But he was not able to. He was certain, however, that he would see him in the Kingdom of God. *" Indeed, I often really wanted to see him personally, but perhaps I was not worthy. But in the Kingdom of Heaven we shall see each other, and all the other holy Fathers, too"*. The same thing was said by Abbas Pimen to his mother, who wanted very much to see him again on earth. As did Saint Symeon the Stylite. While the nun Sophiane, who went to the next world, confesses: *"There I saw my father, the priest Ioannis, and my mother Anastasia, as well as one of my sisters who had died earlier"*.

The question arises: shall the just know those they had already met on earth? Or all the just? Familiar and unfamiliar? The Angel of the Lord said to Saint Makarios of Egypt: *"just as someone goes to the market and sees there people of standing and the poor and asks who this is and who that is, and by questioning learns about those he has never met, the same thing happens there"*. In this way, Saint Andrew the Fool-in-Christ was seeking in Paradise, when he got there, to find the Most Holy Mother of God. (But the saints told him that the Mother of God does not stay in Paradise, but constantly walks the earth).

To the above question there is another answer. The Apostles Peter, John and James recognised Moses and Elijah on Mount Tabor *(Matthew 17, 5)*. But since they did not ask, how did they know who they were? Or how did Saint Sisoes, breathing his last, recognise Saint Anthony, the prophets, the holy apostles? The apostles on Tabor and Saint Sisoes were shining at that moment with the light of Christ. They had a share in the Divine Light. And in this light, in the Lord, the three apostles automatically recognised the prophets. And Saint Sisoes the prophets and the holy apostles. And so, in eternal life, with the light of Christ, each person will recognise the other. *"But even those who never met each other in the flesh in this world"*, writes Saint Symeon the New Theologian, *"will know each other there, for as it is not possible ever for the Father not to recognise the Son, or the Son the Father, likewise the saints, too, when they have become gods by grace, by having God indwelling within them in no way will be unable to recognise each other, but will each see eternally the glory of the other, as the Son sees the glory of the Father and the Father that of the Son"* (Τά Εὑρισκόμενα, p. 230)

2. Those in Hell.

Do they know each other?

The Angel of the Lord replies categorically here: *"The sinners are deprived of this, too"*. The same was said by the pagan priest to Saint Makarios: *"We cannot look anyone in the face. But the back of one is attached to the back of another"*. Precisely because there is no unity in Hell, because there is no love and consequently communication and acquaintance are missing. Hate rules! Evil and enmity! Here on earth, when two people have fallen out and loathe each other mortally, they do not want to see each other. The other's very name, when they hear it, brings on disgust, because of the hatred! In Hell, all this is multiplied a thousand times! *"Hell is the ordeal of not loving anybody"* (Dostoevsky).

3. Do those in Hell see the Just?

"*And in Hades, being in torment, he lifted up his eyes, and saw Abraham, and Lazarus in his bosom*" (Luke XVI, 23). How did the rich man in Hell recognise Abraham? Since he was not a contemporary of his? And since he had no part in the Divine Light. For the rich man in Hell, it was impossible to recognise Abraham the Just. For God, however, it was possible. Because for Him, everything is possible. And God allowed the rich man to see Abraham. To learn from him that his was a just punishment. And that Lazarus was justly enjoying the delights of Paradise. And at the same time to dispel any hope of repentance: "*And besides all this, between us and you a great chasm has been fixed, in order that those who would pass from here to you may not be able, and none may cross from there to us*" (Luke XVI, 26).

Do they, however, see their friends and relations who are in Paradise? Do they recognise them? Does a father, for example, recognise his child? The sight of God is fire for those in Hell. Because they are unworthy to behold the Lord of Glory. And the just will be light "*they shall shine like beacons*" (Matthew 13, 43). Therefore those in Hell will be unworthy to gaze upon them. They would be burned by their brightness.

4. Do the Just recognise those in Hell?

Do the Just recognise those in Hell? If a mother, for example, has a child, and she goes to Paradise. And her child to Hell. Will the mother see the child in Hell? If she does, will she not suffer? And if she does, will Paradise not be Hell? Yes! The Just remember, they know those in Hell.

80

But as God Himself does not feel sorry for those in Hell, neither do the Just. They are at one with God. They become impassive, like God *(Saint Gregory the Dialogist)*.

They recognise now that they are being justly punished. A mother has a child, a sinner, a wastrel, a criminal, a robber. And the child is put in prison. Then the mother, because of her great disappointment in the child, will not be upset deep down, but will rather be relieved. Precisely because her child will have deserved to go to prison! Something similar, but to an incomparably greater extent, happens in the next life. The mother recognises that her child is being punished justly. And is not upset. It is as if it is not her child!...

10. INTERCESSION

1. The Intercessors.

Saint John of the Ladder writes: *"Those who have seen the face of the King and made Him their friend can reconcile, if they want, any servant and helper of His with Him, even if they do not know them or if they are enemies, and can make them enjoy glory. You should think the same of the saints"* (Ladder, ibid. Logos to Pimen). That is to say, the King, for the sake of His friend, glorifies His servants even if the friend does not know them. And more importantly, even if they are enemies. Not because they deserve it, but simply for the sake of the friend. *"You should think the same of the saints".*

For the sake of His saints, God has mercy on, saves, acquits sinners. The saints intercede with God for us and God listens to the prayer. Not that the saints think more carefully than God or are more charitable than Him. Not at all! Simply that God does not want to disappoint them! *"He shall fulfil the desire of those who fear him and their prayer shall be heard"* (Psalm 144, 19).

In Holy Scripture there are numerous examples which show that, for the sake of one person, God saves a whole generation or a whole people.

Rahab hid the spies of Joshua, son of Nun, in her house in Jericho. God was therefore bountiful towards *"her father and her mother and her brothers and her relatives and all those who belonged to her and they were set outside the camp of Israel"* (Joshua VI, 23).

Noah was righteous. And for his sake the whole of his family was saved from the flood. *"And the Lord God said to Noah. Go into the ark, you and all your household, for I have seen you righteous before me in this generation"* (Genesis VII, 1).

Lot resisted sin. And for his sake, God saved all his kindred. *"And the men said to Lot: 'Do you have any brothers-in-law here? Or sons or daughters. If there is anyone of your people in this city, lead them out of this place' "* (Genesis XIX, 12).

Abraham besought God to have mercy on Sodom and Gomorrah. He showed boldness towards the Lord. *"What is this, God? Will you destroy the righteous along with the impious? Are the righteous the same as the impious? And if there are fifty righteous people in the city, will you destroy them? Don't do that. Don't destroy the righteous with the impious"*. Abraham gave a lesson to the Lord, taught Him, admonished Him! And the Lord was not upset by the *"cheek"* of His servant Abraham. And he says to Abraham: *"If there are fifty righteous people in the city, I shall not trouble the whole city for the sake of those fifty"*. And seeing that God is not upset by his forthrightness, Abraham goes on entreating Him, and even more cheekily!. *"And if the righteous are forty-five?"* And the Lord replies: *"No, for their sakes I shall take pity on the city"*. And Abraham asks again: *"What if they're twenty? What if they're ten? What will You do, my*

God? Will You destroy the righteous with the impious?" And to each question of His servant Abraham, the Lord gives the same answer: *"No, but for their sakes I will take pity on the city"*. And the remarkable thing is that Abraham stopped asking the Lord. He did not go down to five! Which is why God departed *(Genesis XVIII, 23-33)*.

God was angry at Israel and wanted to destroy it. But Moses changed God's plans! An ordinary person a servant of ashes, earth, dust was able to alter the plans of the All-wise and All powerful God And God begged Moses *"give me leave"!* Let me destroy Israel! But Moses would not budge. So God changed His plans, He did not do what He had wanted to! *(Exodus XXXII, 9-14)*.

And in the New Testament:

"For the elect...those days shall be shortened" (Matthew 24, 22). For the sake of the elect, the Lord will reduce those grievous days before the Second Coming. So that His elect will not be cast down! In this way, it is a bounty for the whole earth.

The centurion's servant was seriously ill. And he recovered through the intercessions of the centurion *(Matthew 9, 5-13)*.

Hananiah's daughter was possessed and her mother begged the Lord to heal her. *"Then Jesus answered her, 'Woman, your faith is great. Be it done to you as you wish'. And her daughter was healed from that time"* (Matthew 15, 21-8).

The paralytic in Capernaum was made well thanks to the faith of his family. *"And when Jesus saw their faith he said to the paralytic, 'Child, your sins are forgiven'"* (Marc 2,5).

The Apostle Paul was travelling from Crete to Rome when a storm blew up at sea and the boat was in danger of sinking. But thanks to Paul, the whole crew of the ship was saved. The Angel of the Lord told him: *"behold, the Lord has granted you all those sailing with you"* (Acts 27, 24-5).

2. Our intercession for the dead.

God, then, for the sake of one person can save or have mercy on another. It is on this point that we base our prayers for the dead. Various people pray for various others. And for our sakes, God can have mercy on souls. For He is Lord of the souls. *"He who has power over the living and the dead"*... We relatives play the role of lawyer for the defence! And the accused depend for support on their lawyers. If the lawyer is good, the sentence may be reduced! The accused may be acquitted! And we constantly beseech God that the punishment of the souls may be lightened or even that they may be acquitted.

The souls do not pray to leave Hell and go to Paradise. *"In Hades there is no repentance"* (Psalm 6,5. Septuagint version). We pray for the souls. And we do not pray for the souls to go to Paradise. But for God to take them to Paradise! *"With the saints give rest Christ to the souls of Your servants"*. We pray to God. And particularly to God the All-powerful and Lover of Mankind. However much we want somebody to go to Paradise, God wants it infinitely more. Because God has more loving-kindness than we do.

We are not willing to be crucified for our own salvation, how much less for that of our neighbour. God was crucified for our salvation! And that means that He desires our salvation more than we ourselves do. As the Holy Gospel says, Christ healed the sick, He healed the body. Will He not then have mercy on the soul, which is higher than the body? He heeded the entreaty of the demons, who requested that they be not cast into Hell. Will he then not heed a similar entreaty from Christians?

And there is something even more noteworthy: prayers we make for the dead are even more powerful than those we make for the living. Living people have *"free will"*. They decide for themselves what to do. Whether to go to Paradise or not. Nobody forces them, nobody puts them under pressure. Not even God. God simply shows them the ways and means to repentance. And they choose.

But the dead no longer have free will. They are no longer masters of their souls. So it is easier for God to have mercy on a soul. This is why whatever we do for souls is heeded by God! What precisely can our prayers achieve for souls? Two things: the first is that at the exact moment when we pray the soul receives mercy; the second is that the soul can even get out of Hell. And go to Paradise! The first is certain, the second uncertain, but not impossible. *"Alms-giving, liturgies and remembrance services are of great benefit to the soul; they are even able to release it from Hell"* (Revelation of the Angel to Saint Makarios).

The fact that a soul is able to get out of Hell is apparent from the following words of the Lord: *"whoever speaks against the Holy Spirit will not be forgiven, either in this age or in the age to come"* (Matthew 12, 32). That is:

In the next life, only blasphemy against the Holy Spirit (according to the fathers this is unbelief or heresy) is unforgivable. People do not go to Hell only for this sin, but only this one remains unforgivable. It follows, then, that all other sins, however serious they are (!), perhaps can be pardoned. And then the soul will get out of Hell. Why else do we say the *"Thrice-holies"* and the Remembrance Services?

11. WHAT IS PROFITABLE FOR SOULS?

A' Privately.

1. Alms-giving.

Anyone who has real need and is given alms is relieved. And rejoices. And says *"Thank you"* from his or her soul. If, then, people in such a spiritual state pray to God for the person who gave them alms, the prayer has effect before God. This is why we should give alms to those in need and at the same time tell them to obtain forgiveness for such and such a soul. A fisherman, religiously indifferent, gave a poor man a fish. *"Let it be for my niece, Maria"*, he thought, without believing it. The same evening, the dead Maria appeared to the poor man and said to him: *"Tell my uncle that I received the fish, and thank him for it"*.

2. Candles.

We light two candles. One for the living and one for the dead, remembering their names. The candle is a kind of prayer, too. While the candle is burning, it is a time of prayer. Which is why the saints want the whole candle to burn which we place before their icons. So that our prayer will last longer, and so will their intercession for us *(Θησαυρός*

Δαμασκηνού, p.526).

Saint Seraphim of Sarov lit candles for the dead before the icons in his cell, too. Therefore, we can light candles in front of the icons in our homes as well *"in remembrance of the dead"*.

3. Icon-lamps.

The same applies to the icon-lamp which we light on the grave of a deceased person. It is a kind of prayer.

4. Altar-bread, wine and oil.

Whatever we offer the Church for the performance of the Holy Liturgy, all of these, too, help to expiate souls. The nun Sophiane, who went to the next world, relates: *"and the Angels came, bearing the alms, the liturgies, the candles, the oil, the altar-breads...besides, the intercessions of the poor who had received alms were heard, saying 'God forgive you'. Then the voice of the Master was heard, saying: 'Behold, through the prayers of my Priests and my brethren the poor, I grant forgiveness to this soul'"* (Μέγας Συναξαριστής, August, p.112).

5. Prayer.

The pagan priest who was in Hell said to Saint Makarios of Egypt: *"When you show pity on those in Hell and pray for them, they find comfort... seeing, in a way, each others' faces. That is the comfort"*. The saint did not pray especially for the pagan priest, because he did not know of him, but prayed generally for all those in Hell. And it had effect. How much more would a particular prayer have had.

An example:

In 1973, the mother of a monk, Father Seraphim of the Monastery of Saint Paul on the Holy Mountain, died. This monk asked Father Konstantios, a virtuous monk of the same monastery to pray for his mother's soul. Father Konstantios did so for forty days. When this time had passed, Father Konstantios saw in a vision a woman whom he did not know.

- Who are you?, he asked.

- Father Seraphim's mother.

- And what do you want?.

- I came to tell you that through your prayer I found great relief and at the same time I want to thank you for what you did. (Γεροντικό *of the Holy Mountain, vol. II, p. 112)*

Souls are not comforted only temporarily by our personal prayers, but something more bold, more astonishing happens. From Hell they go to Paradise.

In the Life of Saint Thekla there is mention of a widow, Tryphaena, who had a daughter, Falconila, who died and went to Hell. And the dead Falconila said to her mother: *"Mother, love that stranger, Thekla, and have her as your daughter in place of me, because she's a servant of God and can pray and the Lord will put me in the place where the righteous are".* And this indeed happened. Through the prayers of Saint Thekla, Falconila went from Hell to Paradise. (Μέγας Συναξαριστής, *September, pp. 508-511).*

In the Life of Saint Paisios, too, mention is made of a monk who was disobedient and went to Hell. But through the prayers of Saint Paisios he was saved and went to Paradise.

The most astonishing event, however, is described in a book by Archimandrite Kakavelas. In brief, a monk was dining with the Bishop of Kyros, Theodoretos. At table the monk hid his hand with his habit. The Bishop asked the monk why he had his hand covered, pulled the habit aside and uncovered it. An unbearable stench arose. The monk explained: *"My mother was a widow. She was very beautiful and became a harlot. And died. When I realised the vanity of life, I became a monk. But I was extremely concerned as to whether my mother was saved or not. I went to Thebaida to see an elder, a famous ascetic and saint and asked him about it. For seven days the two of us stood and prayed fervently. And in a vision, I saw Hell, and my mother boiling in the cauldrons of Hell. And groaning 'My child, save me!' I snatched her from Hell and put her in Paradise. Then I awoke. And what did I see? My hand, with which I had seized my mother, was injured and stank unbearably, as now. The holy ascetic had the same vision"*.

The conclusion?

Personal prayer on behalf of souls is not wasted. It is certainly beneficial to them. It either relieves them temporarily or even gets them out of Hell. Which is why we have an obligation to pray for our departed brethren. To say *"Lord, have mercy"* for them! What is a *"Lord, have mercy"* to us. A matter of a second. For the soul, however, that second is a treasure! It can even gain eternity!

B' Through the Church.

a. The Church by itself:

By itself the Church is constantly praying for souls.

Every day, morning and evening.

In the Midnight Office: "*Remember Lord, as You are good, Your servants, and forgive them whatever sins they committed in this life...*". "*With the saints give rest, Christ, to the souls of Your servants...*". "*Remember, Lord, our fathers and brethren who have fallen asleep in the hope of the resurrection and eternal life...*". "*Let us esteem...our parents and teachers and all our fathers and brethren who have gone before...*".

At Mattins: "*again we pray for the blessed founders... and for all our fathers and brethren who have gone to their rest before us...*".

At Vespers: As at mattins.

At Compline: "*Let us esteem...our parents and teachers and all our fathers and brethren who have gone before...*" "*Remember Lord all our fathers and brethren who have fallen asleep before us*". And all these prayers are directed to the Creator every day by the Church for the repose of the departed.

Moreover: Every Saturday, at mattins, is chanted a special canon from the Paraclitic and special aposticha of the praises for the repose of the souls.

Saturdays of All Souls: The Church has instituted a special service, (mattins, vespers, divine liturgy) for all the souls from Adam until today: "*again we pray for the blessed memory and eternal repose of all those who have fallen asleep in the hope of the resurrection...from the beginning until the most recent days*". These are the Saturdays of All Souls, of which there are two.

One is the *Saturday before Meat-fare Sunday.* It has symbolic significance, because it precedes the Sunday of

Meat-fare on which the Gospel of the Last Judgement is read. And we entreat God to have mercy on the souls.

The second is the *Saturday before Pentecost*. It is a tradition of the Church that the souls in Hell are free from Easter until Pentecost. The Most Holy Mother of God requested this of the Lord when she was escorted into Hell by the Archangel Gabriel. And the Lord heeded her prayer. At Pentecost, the souls return to Hell, which is why at Vespers for Pentecost the third of the kneeling prayers is especially for the repose of souls. This is how the Saturday of All Souls before Pentecost was instituted. That the Lord would be merciful to the souls which were returning to the place of torment!

At the Holy Liturgy: Souls are remembered at every Liturgy. In particular: at the Offertory, all the dead: *"and of all those, Merciful Lord, our Orthodox fathers and brethren, who have fallen asleep in the hope of the Resurrection of eternal life in communion with You"*.

At the Litany at the Great Entrance: *"and for all our Orthodox fathers and brethren who have fallen asleep before us and who now lie peacefully here and in all other parts of the earth"*.

At the "Holy things to those who are holy": *"and all our fathers and brethren departed before us, may the Lord our God remember..."*.

Immediately after the **"especially our Most Holy ... Lady":** *"And remember all those who have fallen asleep in the hope of the resurrection and of eternal life..."*.

When Saint Makarios, a servant of the Lord, was praying, the souls in Hell were comforted. How much more so now when the whole of the Orthodox Church is praying.

The whole of the Church triumphant and, what is more, day and night. There is a celebration in Hell!

b. We through the Church:

What we offer for the celebration of the Holy Liturgy, altar-breads, candles, incense, oil, wine.

1. Thrice-Holies.

These can be said every day, either at the side of the grave of the deceased or in church before the icon of Christ. And the souls find relief.

Father Dimitris Gagastathis (+1975) relates how in the village of Liopraso, up in the mountains, there lay the bones of four people who had been killed by the resistance in August 1944. He went in the company of some other villagers to collect the bones and put them in the village ossuary. No sooner had they arrived when they heard cries and groans as if people were being tortured at that very moment. The whole company was badly shaken. Father Dimitris read the Thrice-Holy and at once the cries and groans ceased!

Even more noteworthy is the following:

The Emperor Theophilos, who fought against the holy icons, was a heretic and went to Hell. His wife, Theodora, however, begged Patriarch Methodios to pray for his soul. So the patriarch, together with other virtuous members of the clergy prayed fervently in Aghia Sophia for the whole of the first week of Great Lent (During this period they would certainly have said Thrice-Holies and not performed the Divine Liturgy). Likewise, the Empress Theodora prayed with the whole of her court in the Church of the Mother of

God. When Saturday dawned, Theodora saw Christ in a vision! And he said to her: *"Woman, great is your faith. Know, therefore, that through your tears and your faith, and the entreaties of my priests[6] I shall show favour to your husband, Theophilos"*. The miracle happened. The heretic Theophilos was saved. *(Triodion, note to the Saturday before Meat-fare).* This event is recorded in detail by the great Byzantinist Charles Diehl.

2. The Divine Liturgy (Remembrance Services).

The most acceptable sacrifice to God is the Divine Liturgy. Because in it and through it is sacrificed His beloved son for the salvation of the world. God accepts the Divine Liturgy with greater joy than any martyrdom which is endured for His sake. Because through a martyrdom one ordinary person is sacrificed and sanctified. While in the Divine Liturgy, God is sacrificed for the salvation and sanctification of the whole world. This is why the most effective prayer made on behalf of the deceased is the Divine Liturgy. Symeon of Thessaloniki writes: *"Both in the evening and morning, prayers on behalf of the departed do not cease. Then the lawful and customary remembrance services are*

---

6. It seems that the Lord pays heed to the intercessions of priests, more than to any others. In this particular case He said: *"through the intercessions of my priests I will show favour to your husband, Theophilos"*. Sophiane the nun heard the same thing from the lips of the Lord Himself: *"then the voice of the Lord was heard saying 'Behold, through the prayers of my priests ... I grant forgiveness to her' "*. The prayer of the priest is as potent as that of the saints *(Athanasios the Great).*

held, but especially and most importantly the daily blood-
less sacrifice, than which nothing else is so profitable for the
deceased, nor the cause of such joy and enlightenment and
union with God, since the very blood of the Lord is that which
is shed on behalf of us good-for-nothings in this sacrifice,
and the divine Body itself is that which is sacrificed on the
Holy Altar. This sacrifice is offered ceaselessly and every day
by those close to the deceased according to the flesh, those
spiritually united with them and those loving them most, all
the time and for the whole of their lives, and the more they
offer it, the more profitable it is for the deceased, for what
can be more beneficial than Christ being sacrificed for us.

Some offer as much as they can and choose to, while
others furnish this sacrifice and the other lawful remembrance
services every day up to the fortieth at least" ("Ἅπαντα",
Saint Symeon of Thessaloniki, p. 310).

And here are the remarkable results of the Divine
Liturgy.

Saint Gregory the Dialogist relates that a certain
monk, Justus, who was avaricious, fell ill and died. Thirty
consecutive liturgies were said for his soul. And he himself
appeared one night to his brother after the flesh, Capiosus.
The latter immediately asked him how he was getting on
there. *"So far it has been terrible, but now it's fine"*. Capiosus
at once came to the monastery and divulged the dream to
us. When we had reckoned up the days exactly, we found
that indeed, on that very day, the thirtieth liturgy for the
soul of the departed brother had been held (Εὐεργετινός, vol.
II, p. 109).

And even more astonishing:

Saint Gregory the Dialogist said forty liturgies for the

repose of the soul of the persecutor of the Church, Trajan *(P. G. vol.95, 256C-264A)*. And God heard his petition and brought Trajan out of hell. God then reprimanded the saint, however, and told him not to pray for the impious again *(Triodion, note for the Saturday before Meat-fare)*. God reprimanded the saint after Trajan had left Hell! Not before. Oh, what Mercy!

Does this seem strange to us? These amazing events? Is not now, the period until the Second Coming of the Lord, a time of mercy for the living and the dead? Why should the mercy of the Lord be confined to Paradise? Is it not infinite?

12. WHAT IS HARMFUL FOR SOULS?

For the sake of one person, God will save another, or even a whole people. The converse is also true, however. Because of one person, a group of others or even a whole people can be punished and sent to Hell *"visiting the sins of the fathers upon the children to the third and fourth generation of those who hate me" (Exodus 20, 5).*

Solomon sinned. *"And King Solomon was fond of women and he had seven hundred wives, princesses, and three hundred concubines and he took foreign wives" (I Kings 11, 1).* God became angry and Solomon had to be punished. But since his father David had been God-fearing, he was not punished. God *"withheld"* his punishment until after Solomon's death. And, indeed, on his death, his kingdom was divided. Punishment came. Solomon was to blame, but his children paid for it!

Ahab, the King of Israel, murdered Naboth and seized his vineyard. The Lord was angered and, through the mouth of the Prophet Elijah, foretold Ahab's appalling end. Ahab was devastated and repented. So the Lord took back His word and did not punish him. But He punished his children! *"And the Lord said 'Have you seen how Ahab has humbled himself before me? I will not bring the evil in his days, but in the days of his son will I bring the evil'"* (I Kings 20, 29). Ahab sinned, and his children were punished.

The Israelites were unable to capture the city of Ai. They were in despair, utterly cast down. The cause? Achar had stolen silver from Jericho and hidden it in his tent *(Joshua, chapter VII)*. One person sinned, and a whole people was punished.

Jonah transgressed the Lord's commandment. Instead of going to Nineveh, he took ship and went to Tarshish. A storm blew up. The crew were terrified and the ship was on the point of sinking. But as soon as Jonah was thrown into the sea, the wind dropped *(Jonah, chapter I)*.

A very similar case is that of Saint John the Evangelist. Because he was less than happy at going to preach the Gospel in the difficulties of Asia, the ship on which he was travelling was tossed on the waves for forty days, while the whole crew suffered *(Μέγας Συναξαριστής, September, p. 558)*.

So, just as, for the sake of one, another is saved, or even a whole people, by the same token, because of one person a number of people or even whole nations may be punished. And just as for our sakes, souls are granted mercy, bounties and salvation, in the same way, through us, they suffer. They even go to Hell. We do not affect them only positively, but negatively, too.

Let us look at this:

The servant of God, Eleftheria, as we have already said, was in torment because she had been buried in a Turkish grave-yard. Although her soul was in Paradise, it was suffering! The rich worldly man had a magnificent funeral, but lost his soul through it. Who buried the servant of God, Eleftheria, in a Turkish grave-yard? Who gave the rich man the magnificent funeral? Their families and relatives. That is to say that they, in their ignorance, were the cause of the souls coming to harm.

The following case is also relevant:

The blessed, late Father Philotheos Zervakos related how he went to take a couple's confession. They had lost their only child, a daughter, a God-fearing student of Theology whom they had loved dearly. The wife bore up bravely under the blow of the death. She lit the icon-lamp in the house and prayed. The husband was completely the opposite. He shut himself up in the house, blasphemed Christ and blew out the icon-lamp. One day, however, he fell into ecstasy. He went to Paradise. And there saw his daughter. He was astonished, because, although she was in Paradise, in a beautiful land, dressed as a bride, she was bitter galled.

- What's the matter, daughter? Here you are in the midst of joy, but you're not rejoicing.

- Father, how can I rejoice at what you're doing? Blaspheming Christ?

- So, it's my fault you're not happy?

Then the husband woke up, thoroughly shaken and overjoyed! He had a shave, dressed in his best, and went out shopping for the first time since the death of his daughter. People gave him their condolences. And he answered *"No, I want congratulations!"*

So that is how relatives on earth can harm souls in Heaven.

Let us be careful when someone close to us dies. Otherwise, there is the fear, the danger of harming their soul. Let us become better, for our own benefit and for that of our departed brethren.

An inspired ascetic from the Holy Mountain has said: *"The best remembrance service for our deceased is our repentance"*.

13. THE LORD'S SECOND COMING

1. Our insensibility.

If suddenly we were to hear the terrible news of war, we would be overcome by anxiety, fear, terror, agitation, because our lives would be in danger, because we might be lost. We would be right to be agitated.

There is, however, something more terrible than war! And more devastating. The Second Coming of the Lord. It is certain to happen. And certain that we shall have to give an account of all our works, words and thoughts from the time of our birth to that of our death.

This is the scandal:

We are Christians. We fear the war which is not certain to come about, and if it does we are not sure to be killed. We do not fear the Second Coming, which is certain to come about and at which we shall have to give an account. Although we are Christians, we are spiritually dead, because we are dominated by considerations of the flesh, by the fear that we shall lose this life, not eternal life.

And fear of the Judgement is apparent when a Christian stops sinning, *"in deed, word and thought"*. Otherwise this fear is false and therefore not fear. Fearlessness is the product either of insensibility or boldness. This is why

Anthony the Great dared say *"I no longer fear the Lord"*. *"In this is love perfected in us, that we may have boldness on the day of Judgement"* (I John 4, 17). Because *"there is no fear in love, but perfect love casts out fear"* (I John 4, 18).

2. When will the Lord come?

"The Lord is not slow about his promise as some count slowness, but is forbearing towards you, not wishing that anyone should perish, but that all should come to repentance" (II Peter 3, 9). As long as we live there is hope of salvation. And because the Lord wants us to be saved, he extends our lives. *"But of that day and the hour no one knows, not even the angels of heaven, nor the Son, but the Father only"* (Matthew 24, 36). Does the Lord not know when He will return? Careful study of chapter 24 (verses 3-42) of the Gospel according to Saint Matthew reveals that the Lord does know when He will return. When He says that before then there will be wars, famine, earthquakes in various places *"but all this is only the onset of labour"* (Matthew 24, 8), this shows that He has some knowledge. *"How can He Who says that, near the end, these signs shall appear in the heavens and the parts of the earth, know nothing of the end? For by this He says 'The end is not yet', not as one who doubts, but knowingly defining it"*. (Basil the Great, letter 236, to Amphilochios the Bishop). So the Lord knows the time of His Second Coming. *"Through identity of being and indissoluble union the soul of the Lord was enriched with knowledge of future events as well as the other wonders. We call Him Master and Lord of all Creation, the one Christ, identical with both God and Man, and seeing all things"* (Saint John of Damascus, The Precise Exposition of the Orthodox

Faith, 21, on ignorance and servitude).

Saint John Chrysostom *(Homily 20 on Matthew)* says the same. As does the hymnology of the Church *"Who but You knows Your Father? Who but You knows the hour and the day? For in You are all the treasures of wisdom, Christ our God"* *(Triodion, Great Monday evening, Compline, ode 9).* It is as if the Lord is saying, *"I know when I shall come again, but I do not wish to tell you. Because it is not in your interests to know. There is a danger of you becoming indolent".*

But the world continues to be ridden by wars, famine and earthquakes. From the time of Christ until now. Signs of the Second Coming. And the Lord, of course, knew all that in advance. And still He has not returned! This is out of love for mankind. So that He will always be close. He is coming! *"I come soon" (Revelation 22, 20).* Which is why we should always be expecting Him.

The holy Fathers *"prophecy"* the day when the Lord will return. *"And evening fell and the morning came, one day" (Genesis I, 5).* Why does it not say *"the first day"*, since other days followed. But it says *"one day"*. As if it were the only one in Creation? This day is an icon of the age to come. The future day without evening. The one and only *(Basil the Great, homily II, 41 on the six days).* On the first day of Creation, light was divided from the darkness. And there was light. This is what will happen on the day of the re-creation of the world, on the day of the Second Coming. The light will be separated from the darkness. And there will be one day. The eighth. The one and only.

The first day of Creation is Sunday, the Lord's day. The Revelation of Saint John the Evangelist was written on a Sunday. The Annunciation of the Mother of God took place on a Sunday. On a Sunday, Christ was born. On a Sunday, He rose from the dead. And the general resurrection of the dead will take place on a Sunday. *"In the new grace, that holy and welcome day is called The Lord's Day, because on it the main events of the Lord's life took place, such as the Annunciation, the Nativity of the Lord, His Resurrection, and the general resurrection of the dead is going to take place on it. Perceptible light was created by God on it, says John of Damascus, and again, that on this day the Lord's Coming is to be expected, so that for boundless ages this one day, the eighth, will remain, as being outside these seven ages, which have day and night"* (Philokalia, Saint Peter of Damascus).

3. How will the Second Coming occur?

a. Nature.

Holy Scripture writes about turmoil in nature, or rather the destruction of nature. *"And I shall give portents in the heavens above and signs on the earth beneath, blood and fire and columns of smoke. The sun shall be turned to darkness and the moon to blood before the day of the Lord comes, the great and manifest day "* (Joel and Acts 2, 19-20). And again: *"The day of the Lord will come like a thief, and then the heavens will pass away with a loud noise and the elements dissolved with fire, and the earth and the works that are on it will be burned up"* (II Peter 3, 10). And the hymnology of our Church: *"Let us attend to what the Creator of all cries: 'Woe to those who desire to see the terrible day of the Lord; for it is darkness; all things shall be tried in the fire'"* (Burial Service).

b. Why all these terrible things?

Nature was polluted by Adam's sin. And it continues to be so through the sins of Adam's descendants. Which is why it has revolted against mankind. That is, it has changed its form! Before the Fall of Adam, for instance, there was no winter, no torrential rain *(Saint John of Damascus, ibid., Concerning the earth and what it bears)*. These, and much else, came after the Fall, as a protest by nature against sinful man! *"For the creation was subjected to futility, not of its own will, but by the will of him who subjected it in hope...We know that the whole creation has been groaning in travail together until now" (Romans 8, 20-22)*.

And now, in the Second Coming, it is cleansed; the decay of sin is burned by Divine Fire. Just as nature was made first, then mankind, so now nature is renewed first, then mankind *(Saint Symeon the New Theologian, Τά Εὑρισκόμενα, p.212)*. *"For creation waits with great longing for the sons of God to be revealed... because creation will be set free from its bondage to decay and obtain the glorious liberty of the children of God" (Romans 8, 19-22)*.

So terrible will the sight of the burning of all things be, that even the angelic powers will be shaken *"And the powers of the heavens will be shaken" (Matthew 24, 30)*. How much more so will mankind be! *"Who shall stand, Lord, the dreadful threat of Your Coming. There the heavens will be rolled up like a terrible book and the stars fall, creation be shaken with fear and light changed" (Burial Service)*. *"And then the sign of the Son of man shall appear in the heaven" (Matthew 24, 24)*. And this sign is the Cross of the Lord *(Saint Ephraim the Syrian, Ἀσκητικά, p. 33)*. *"The sun shall* be turned to darkness and the moon to blood" (Acts 2, 19). That is, darkness will fall. And how then will the Cross appear? How will it be visible, up there in the heavens, by those who inhabit the earth? The Cross, as the glory of the Lord, shines! It flashes! Glory means light, not darkness.

Christ is the King. The King has a sceptre, a symbol of His authority, of His power. The sceptre of the Lord is the Cross, *"the rod of power"* (Psalm 109, 2). And when the King walks abroad, the sceptre precedes Him. The same here. First the sceptre, the Cross, and then the King, Christ!

And His Coming will be so overwhelming, the Cross, *"and all the angels with him"* (Matthew 24, 32), that *"every knee shall bow, in the heavens, on earth and among the dead"* (Mattins prayer). And then *"we shall be caught up in the clouds to meet the Lord in the air"* (I Thessalonians 4, 17), which declares our transfiguration (Blessed Kallistos, Philokalia), *"and thus we shall always be in the Lord"* (I Thessalonians, ibid.).

4. How will the Lord judge?

How do we judge? Influenced by the passions we have within us. Therefore we do not judge clearly, neither fairly nor unfairly! How does the Lord judge? Impassionately. Therefore clearly and fairly. Since we have passions and restricted powers of reason, we do not understand the judgement of the Lord. It is a towering mountain, hard of access, or rather, entirely inaccessible. *"Your righteousness is like the mountains of God, your judgements like the great deep"* (Psalm 35, 7).

"Judge me, Lord, according to my righteousness" (Psalm 7, 9). Judge me, Lord according to my weakness, to my

capabilities. Do not ask anything more of me. *"And do not enter into judgement with your servant, for in your sight shall no man living be justified" (Psalm 142, 2)*. Because if You judge normally, in accordance with Your demands, everyone will be guilty in Your sight! *"Judge me, Lord, according to your judgement" (Psalm 34, 24)*. Judge me, Lord, according to Your judgement. Your mercies and Your compassion.

Let us at this point listen to the voice of Abbas Dorotheos: *"It is for God alone to justify and to condemn, He Who knows the circumstances and the potential, the reversals and the gifts, the temperament and the skills and Who judges each as He alone knows. For God judges differently the sins of the Bishop and those of the eminent citizen; those of the abbot and the school-child differently; those of the old man and the youth differently; those of the sick and those of the healthy differently. And who can know all the judgements of God, save He alone, Who made all things and knows all things!" (Abbas Dorotheos, Κατανυκτικοί Λόγοι, p. 54)*.

And he asks: *"Will God judge the young woman who was raised in a licentious environment, and sins, in the same way as one who was raised and cared for in a Christian environment, and sins?"* And he answers: *"Certainly not!"*. That is, God will take everything into account, each person's environment, knowledge, age, judgement, nature, disposition, will and understanding. The Lord Himself said to Saint Pachomios: *"In the last times, those who, without examples and leaders, struggle to save their souls will be given the reward of a great athlete"*. Which is why a very spiritual contemporary Athonite ascetic says: *"In Paradise there'll be some surprises"*.

On the day of Judgement, all those healthy people

who did not put their health to good use, will envy and be jealous of the sick who bore their sicknesses in a way pleasing to God! Sighted people will envy the blind, the able-bodied will be jealous of the halt and the lame. Those who are intelligent and wise, but did not put their wisdom to good use will be envious and jealous of the stupid and the mad, precisely because they will be judged leniently and will gain Paradise. This is why Saint Arsenios of Cappadocia gave a blessing in disguise to an impious woman, who was given to blasphemy and pride, that is, that she should lose her mind, go mad, so that she would be judged by God as a little child and that her soul would be saved.

The Gospel for the Sunday of Meat-fare: In this Gospel *(Matthew 25, 31-46)*, the Lord is not at all demanding. All He asks is a basic standard of virtue. Have we fed the hungry, slaked the thirst of the thirsty, clothed the naked, visited the sick? Something that even non-Christians manage to do with ease. No matter how callous people are, they will have pity on any hungry person they come across. They will have pity on anyone they see naked in winter. If one of their family or friends is sick, they will visit them.

But Christ Himself said that whoever calls his brother a fool, *"shall be liable to the fire of Gehenna" (Matthew 5, 22)*.

"Do not judge, that you be not judged" (Matthew 7, 1).

We shall be accountable for every careless word on the Day of Judgement *(Matthew 12, 36)*.

If we do not forgive, we shall not be forgiven *(Matthew 6, 14-15)*.

If you look at a woman with desire, you commit adultery *(Matthew 5, 28)*.

Sodom and Gomorrah will be judged with greater leniency than those who deny the word of God *(Luke 10, 12)* and so on.

Why then, does He overlook all this, and much else besides, on the Day of Judgement?

Christ has before Him all the nations of the earth. That is, nations who have heard but a little, or nothing at all about Christ. Nations without preachers of the word of God, without churches, without priests, without scriptures, idolatrous nations. And it follows that they are in ignorance of all this. Which is why they themselves are at a loss! When did they see Christ naked, hungry, sick, imprisoned and were indifferent? They did not know that what we do to our neighbour applies to Christ. This is why Christ demands from them a basic standard of virtue. But for Christians, who know the Scriptures, the Judgement will be different, strict. For them it is not enough to give a piece of bread, or a glass of water and to get to Paradise on the strength of them. If they do not forgive their neighbour, how will they get to Paradise? And so on. *"From everyone to whom much has been given, much will be required, and of those to whom much has been committed much more will be demanded"* *(Luke 12, 48)*.

The Gospel of the last Judgement has a double explanation for the Christian. First: material concern for the poor. Second: spiritual concern for the soul, one's own and one's neighbour's. As if the Lord were saying: *"Your soul was thirsty and you did not feed it with the word of God. It was denuded of virtues and you did not clothe it. It was sick with sin and you did not heal it. It was imprisoned by the passions and you did not release it! 'Since I was hungry for your return',* says Saint Symeon the New Theologian, *"and for your repentance and you did not give me anything to eat, and to satisfy my desire, therefore, you did not repent of your evil. I was thirsty for your salvation, and you did not give me anything to drink. I was denuded of your virtuous acts and you did not clothe me with them. I was in the narrow, polluted and dark prison of your heart and you did not wish to visit me and let me out into the Light. You saw how I lay sick with the illness of your own neglect and inaction and you did not serve me with your good deeds. Well, then, begone from me"* (Saint Symeon the New Theologian, ibid., p. 296).

14. CONCERNING PARADISE

1. The Foretaste

Paradise is participation in the life of God, which comes by keeping His law. Observing the commandments of the Lord, even the least of these, brings peace and joy to the soul. *"Glory and honour and peace to everyone who does good" (Romans 2, 10).*

A contemporary, very spiritual monk on the Holy Mountain writes: *"If people would examine the spiritual benefit and inner joy which they feel in this world from even a small act of goodness towards their neighbour, they would beg the neighbour to accept it and would, furthermore, be grateful. Because the alteration which a soul undergoes and the joy felt by the heart of a charitable person cannot be given by the greatest cardiologist, even if you pay him a sackful of money. In just the same way, the joy felt by Christians engaged in the struggle, who keep vigils, pray and fast cannot be imagined by those who eat what they like and drink wines and other refreshments"* (Ὁ Γέρων Χατζη-Γεώργιος ὁ Ἀθωνίτης, p. 72).

"The fruit of the spirit is love, joy, peace, patience, kindness, goodness, faithfulness, gentleness, self-control" (Galatians 5, 22). If we observe the law of God, then the

"fruit of the spirit", which is the foretaste of Paradise, enters into the soul. The foretaste of a meal does not come through the imagination or thought, nor through desire, the eyes or the ears, but only through the special sense of taste. In the same way, the foretaste of Paradise comes only through the special sense of taste: the observance of the Divine Commandments. *"Taste and see that the Lord is good"* (Psalm 33, 9). Live according to His will and you will see that *"the Lord is good"*. The psalmist did not say *"eat your fill"*, but *"taste"*. Because repletion belongs to the next age. *"I shall be filled with the sight of your glory"* (Psalm 16, 15).

In the Life of Saint Seraphim we read:

" - I feel such peace and tranquillity in my soul that I cannot express in any word.

- That, friend of God, (explained the saint) is the peace of which the Lord spoke to His disciples: 'My peace I give you; not as the world gives do I give to you' (John 14, 27).

- What else do you feel?

- A strange, unknown delight.

- Yes, that is how it is with those delights which the psalmist describes: 'They will feast on the abundance of your house, and you will give them drink from the torrents of your delights' (Psalm 35, 8)... *We both feel such ineffable blessedness that melts our heart, a blessedness that is beyond words. What more do you feel?*

- An amazing happiness fills my heart".

Father Seraphim went on: *"When the Holy Spirit of God descends on a person and envelops them with the plenitude of His presence, then the soul of that person is filled with ineffable joy, because the Holy Spirit makes everything He touches jubilant"* (Life of Saint Seraphim).

A certain other contemporary ascetic, a servant of God, seems to have had a similar experience. Here is how he describes it: *"It was two hours to sunset, and, while I was reading, Father Arsenios visited me. And like a teacher patting a pupil who has done well at his lessons, he did the same to me. At the same time, he left me with an inexpressible sweetness and heavenly exultation in my heart, which it was impossible for me to bear. I ran outside around my hut afterwards like a madman and kept calling for him, because I thought I would find him. (Fortunately no visitor arrived, because he would have been worried and I would have been unable to tell him the cause of this divine madness and to reassure him). Sometimes I would shout loudly: 'My Father, my Father!' And at other times I would cry more softly: 'My God, my God, hold my heart a little tightly till I see what is going to happen tonight!' Because it would have been impossible for my heart of clay to stand that great sweetness of Paradise, had it not been for God's help"* (Saint Arsenios of Cappadocia, p. 41 [English translation])[7].

7. In the body of earth and clay the beauty of Paradise! That is a miracle! *"We have this treasure in earthen vessels, to show that the transcendent power belongs to God, not to us"* (2 Corinthians 4, 7). The body is unable to bear the beauty of the life of incorruption, because it is perishable. Decay does not inherit immortality (I Corinthians 15, 50). If all Christians felt this heavenly sweetness, they would fall into total inertia! At the same time, they would beg God to be allowed to leave this world as quickly as possible, as did Symeon the Just, on taking Jesus into his arms: *"Now Lord let your servant depart"* (Luke 2, 29). He felt himself a captive. Bound. Imprisoned. Because for those who desire the life above, their sojourn

And this joy, however great it is, is no more than a foretaste! Saint Seraphim said to his disciple, Motovilov: *"But however comforting this joy is which you now feel in your soul, it is nothing compared to that which the Lord has prepared 'for those who love him'. We are now being given a foretaste of that joy. And if now we feel such joy and gladness in our hearts, what shall we say about that joy which He has prepared in heaven for those who labour here on earth!"* (Life of Saint Seraphim).

Indeed! If that is the foretaste, what will repletion be like! The human mind cannot conceive what Paradise will be like. *"What no eye has seen, nor ear heard, nor the heart of man conceived, what God has prepared for those who love Him"* (I Corinthians 2, 9).

2. Paradise - the Vision of God.

The Apostle Paul *"was caught up into heaven and heard things that cannot be told, which no-one can utter"* (2 Corinthians 12, 4). Saint Symeon the New Theologian, expanding on the theology of this scriptural passage, tells us that *"the things that cannot be told"* are nothing other than the Most Holy Body of the Lord. The Son of God our Father Himself. Paradise, then, is the vision of God! *"Face to face"* (I Corinthians 13, 12). *"And his servants shall worship him and see his face"* (Revelation, 22,2). The Lord says: *"The angels forever gaze upon the face of my father in heaven"* (Matthew 18, 10): because they do not have material

---

here is the greatest punishment and imprisonment. *(Saint Basil the Great, Homily on the martyr Julita, 5, 5).*

bodies, a hindrance to seeing God. Thus, just as the angels *"forever gaze upon the face of God"*, so shall the righteous look forever upon the Lord in the age to come: because the material body will become spiritual *(I Corinthians 15, 35)*.

It is impossible, from this life, to understand what the vision of God means, because of the body. *"Now we are separated from the vision of the glorious Epiphany through the disabling sickness of the body in which we find ourselves" (Basil the Great, Homily on Psalm 33, 11, 16).* *"For now we see dimly, as in a mirror, but then face to face" (I Corinthians 13, 12).*

3. Vision of the Cross.

"When the Son of Man comes in His glory" (Matthew 25, 31). The Glory of the Lord is His Loving-kindness. The embodiment of His Loving-kindness is the Cross. *"We give thanks to You for Your great glory".* We give thanks to Him for the condescension which has been shown for our sakes- for the Cross!

It follows that the Lord will come *"in His glory"*. He will come with the trophy of the Cross! And, of course, the glory of the Lord, the Cross, will always be in the sight of the righteous [but not of the impious, *"let the impious be carried off, so that they do not see the glory of the Lord" (Isaiah 26, 10)].* It will be planted in the very centre of Paradise, as was the tree of life, so that the souls of those who were saved through the Cross will be illumined. Moreover, the righteous, the victors over sin, over the Devil and over the world will have as their boast, as their trophy, the sign of the Cross! *"And his name shall be on their foreheads" (Re-velation 22, 4),* meaning *"the sign of the Lord" (Abbas Isaiah,*

Εὐεργετινός, vol.II, p. 466). The Cross!

4. Paradise - the Choirs of the Saints.

"In my father's house there are many rooms" (John 14, 1). All the righteous will not enjoy the same glory - *"a star differs from another star in glory"* (I Corinthians 15, 41). *"By 'many rooms', the Saviour refers to the different ways of ascent and advancement to the state there; for the Kingdom is one, but with many differences within it, so that all may shine in the one divine firmament"* (Saint Gregory of Sinai, Philokalia).

In the age to come, says Saint Isaak the Syrian, all will live in one and the same place, undivided, illumined by a noetic sun according to their measure, and will enjoy grace and gladness as from one and the same air, and place and seat and vision and form. But each does not see the measure of the other, neither those above nor those below, so that they will not be saddened at the sight of the greater amount of grace shown to their friends, and their own relative deficiency *(Logos 56)*.

5. Progress of the Righteous.

"They shall go on from strength to strength" (Psalm 83, 8). That is, the righteous. As they are continuously illumined here, so they advance in the next life. Advancement all the time. *"In which we never reach the end of advancement, not even in the life to come, by light receiving the light of knowledge"* (Saint John of the Ladder, Logos 26, B, 38). The same is also true for the angels *(ibid.)*. Saint Gregory of Sinai writes concerning this, that: *"In the future, the Angels and saints, they say, never cease to advance in terms of adding*

118

to their gifts, nor do they give up the merits they have at their command; for that age does not have diminution or reduction of virtue to evil" (Philokalia).

Can anyone, then, comprehend the joy and gladness of the righteous in the age to come. The mind reels! Is eternal life endless? Then so, too, is the progress of the righteous. And so, too, is their joy.

And the strange thing is this:

Although they will advance eternally, and their enlightenment will increase eternally, they will never reach the Light of Christ, nor be identified with it! It will always be far-off. Eternally. Because the Lord is always unapproachable. *"He alone has immortality, dwelling in unapproachable light, whom no-one has seen, or is able to see"* (I Timothy 6, 16).

15. CONCERNING HELL

1. The Foretaste.

Hell is life without God. Far from God. Therefore, it does not begin after death, but before it. In this present life.

Do people live in sin? This is a foretaste of Hell. What is Hell? Fear. Terror. Anguish. Despair. Distress. Sorrow. Sighing. And what is sin? Fear. Terror. Despair. Distress. Sorrow. Sighing: Just what Hell is. *"There will be tribulation and distress for all the souls of people who do evil (Romans 2, 9).* There are no exceptions in sin! *"For all the souls of people"*, tribulation and distress.

When Cain killed his brother Abel, God told him *"You will lament and tremble on the earth"* (Genesis 4, 12). The dreadful experience and cry of the sinner. Only the sinner feels it, and only God hears. Jean-Paul Sartre, well-known for his atheism and therefore his prodigality, lived this tragedy of sin. Here is how he himself, tragically and graphically, describes his secret torment: *"I will put up with anything, the flaming pincers, the boiling lead, the spits, the strangulations - all the Satanic engines you have, whatever scalds, skins and tears. I will bear any torture you perform. Anything is preferable to this anguish of the soul, this lingering pain which eats at a man, sears him and never strikes*

hard enough to finish him off" (Sartre, Huis Clos). Terrible
words! He agrees to put up with anything, any kind of bodily torment, so long as he is delivered from the pain of his
soul. And Sartre is certainly expressing the experience of
all sinners. Unless the rest of them are without souls...There
is, then, no way that Sartre can bear this spiritual torment, which is a foretaste of Hell. And if he is terrified by a
drop of water, how will he react when faced by a boundless
ocean? Which is why the Lord said of Judas, who was going
to Hell *"it would have been better for that man not to have
been born"* (Matthew 26, 24). And Saint Makarios of Egypt
"Woe to the day on which a person is born".

2. Hell-Conscience.

"Every man's conscience is a thousand swords"
(Shakespeare, Richard III). Swords are controls, remorse
which comes from the act of sin. Which is why sins are
unforgettable. An old woman, a hundred years old, might
forget what she ate an hour before. But she remembers
very well, in every detail, the sins she committed in her
younger days. She remembers because they are a repri-
mand to her.

But because people sin all the time, their consciences
are riddled, are buried. So they hear the voice of conscience
faintly, if at all. And they relax. On their death, however,
the conscience awakes, becomes active. It is freed from neglect, indolence, contempt, and most of all from the prison
of the body, and becomes a knife which stabs at the soul.
It makes people see not only the great, mortal sins, but also
the little, tiny ones! Deeds, words, thoughts, imaginings.
And all these, which are uncountable, are stabwounds for

the soul!

And something else:

There is no comparison between the examination performed by the conscience here on earth and that after death. Before death, the soul is embedded in the flesh, covered over, wrapped up in the concerns of life. After death it is liberated from these, and, once free, reprimands people most severely.

Let us hear what the Blessed Dorotheos has to say:

"For the soul wars against this body with the passions and is comforted, eats, drinks, sleeps, talks to and meets up with friends. But when it leaves the body it is left alone with the passions. It is tormented by them, at odds with them, incensed at being troubled by them and savaged by them...Do you want an example of what I'm saying to you? Let one of you come and let me lock him up in a dark cell, and for no more than three days let him not eat nor drink, nor sleep, not meeting anyone, not singing hymns nor praying, not even desiring God, and you will see what the passions make of him. And that while he is still in this life. How much more so when the soul has left the body and is delivered to the passions and will remain all alone with them. What will the miserable soul then suffer? " (Our Blessed Father Abbas Dorotheos, Κατανυκτικοί Λόγοι, pp. 90-1).

And these are the fires of Hell! *"The souls burn with the fire of conscience"* (Gregory the Dialogist). *"I am in anguish in this flame"* (Luke 16, 25). These are the nails, the cauldrons, the instruments of torture of Hell.

Hell for the Christian:

If two people both live the same sort of sinful life, and

one of them is unbaptised and the other a baptised Christian, Hell for the Christian will be more painful. Because for him the pangs of conscience will strike deeper, because of baptism *(The Ladder 26, III, 55)*. It follows, then, that the torments of Hell will be greater! The idolatrous priest in Hell told Saint Makarios: *"As high as the heavens are from the earth, so deep is the fire beneath us and we stand in fire from head to foot...There is greater torture beneath us...We, because we did not know God, find a certain amount of mercy. Those who knew Him, however, and rejected Him or did not do His will are below us".*

3. Hell - God - Fire.

There are no fires, only people's actions, and also the Presence of God. That is a different trial! God is *"Fire" (Deuteronomy 4, 24)*. And fire has two properties. It burns and illumines. God as fire illumines the Righteous. And He burns the sinners. *"For all those who do evil hate the light" (John 3, 20)*. The sinners hate the light. God. And are therefore burned by hatred. By God. Their tragic spiritual state makes them hate not only the Light, God, but everything that has any connection with the Light. Churches, priests, Christians. While sinners walk past psychiatric hospitals calmly and quietly, outside churches they are horrified and shudder. Outside prisons containing the worst elements of society, criminals, robbers, kidnappers, murderers they walk calmly and quietly, while outside churches they are horrified and shudder. Why? After all, the prisons are only concrete, as are the churches. Because of their sins and their tragic spiritual state, churches are a reminder for them of God, Whom they hate. And at the same time they are a

124

challenge to them to repent. And because they do not want to repent, they are horrified and shudder. While Sartre was living in Paris, he complained to the mayor about the church bells annoying him. When such a soul, then, leaves the world with such hatred towards God and enters the next life, this hatred is exacerbated. The fire blazes.

Those in Hell in the next life hate God to an unbearable extent. And simultaneously feel the absurdity that they cannot do without Him. Because the soul, as the breath of God, is starved without Him. Never mind if it does not love Him, even if it hates Him it still seeks Him. Nietsche, that great abjuror of God felt how absurd this life is. He said to God: *"Come back! Even with the lash! Come back! The tears in my eyes flow for You! My heart seeks You. It burns for You! Come back, my Unknown, my God. Come back my Heart, my last Hope"*. And the famous rich man, Dives, in the parable, who is in anguish in Hell does not beg Abraham for water, but for God. He asks for a little Grace. The least amount of Grace to cool him. *"He thirsts for a drop of grace, as Dives without mercy"* (Triodion, Wednesday before Palm Sunday, Aposticha of the Praises).

And here is the terrible thing. This aversion to God is the most awful torment for those in Hell! *"For the alienation from and aversion to God is more unbearable and burdensome to the sufferer than the things to be expected in Hell in general"* (Basil the Great, *"Ὅροι κατά πλάτος"*, II, 2, 13). So there are two torments. Two fires. Sinful deeds and the Presence of God!

4. Everlasting Damnation and the Justice of God.

Hell is eternal. *"And they shall be sent into eternal*

damnation" *(Matthew 25, 46)*. The Angel of the Lord told Saint Makarios: *"If someone had to remove grains of sand for a thousand years from the sea and put them somewhere else, he would have some hope of finishing, but the damnation of the sinners has no end"*.

We often hear:

"Is it fair for sinners to be condemned eternally?"

Just as it is fair for righteous to rejoice eternally, so it is for sinners to be punished eternally.

Hell is not the creation of God, but of the Devil. And it is not for people, but for the Devil, *"for the devil and his angels" (Matthew 25, 41)*. And it is for the Devil because he cannot repent. And he cannot repent because he has no body, only spirit, while people can repent because they have bodies *(Saint John of Damascus, ibid. 3 (17) On Angels)*.

Hell is not God's punishment for people, but self-punishment by people. They punish themselves because they transgress God's law. And this trespass has punishment as its natural consequence. This is why God did not say to the First-created that on the day they ate He would kill them, but that *"you will die unto death"*, you will die by yourselves.

Now here is the question:

Is it fair or reasonable that for a sin lasting a few minutes people should be sent to Hell for ever?

The answer is this:

How long does a murder take? A second. But no lawyer ever says in court: *"You know, the murder took only a second to commit, so the punishment ought to last a second, as well"*! But the accused is tried and sentenced to life imprisonment. What does life mean? As long as they live. The

126

same in the next life. Sinners are punished for life. As long as they live. In fact, it is probably more flexible here. Have you sinned? You are given the chance to repent. And to be acquitted completely. You get no such chance in a court of law. And besides, here the Judge is not a person, but the Merciful God, incomparably more Merciful and Just than earthly judges.

Or suppose somebody is travelling by car and at some point stops concentrating. He or she jerks the wheel and an accident happens. They are badly injured. Paralysed. There is no cure and they remain paralysed for life. For as long as they live. Fifty, a hundred, a thousand years, as long as Methuselah lived, they are paralysed. How long did the jerk of the wheel last? A second. And yet because of a second, they are tortured for life. The same is true about eternal life. Here, too, things are more flexible. Have you sinned? You are given the chance of repenting. You lost concentration for a second and an accident happened? You are not given the chance of restoring your health.

In the end, stupid people go to Hell. Is it not stupidity when you know that Hell exists and you sin for a moment and do not repent as long as you live? This is why the Lord in His anger addresses those about to go to Hell *"Depart from me, you who are accursed" (Matthew 24, 41)*, furious at their utter foolishness. Which is why the Lord does not force anybody to follow Him. *"Whosoever wishes" (Mark 8, 34)*. Because it is such a simple matter, so simple that there is no need for the Lord to force us and beg us to avoid Hell and go to Paradise. We just have to understand it for ourselves and force ourselves. *"Men of violence will take the Kingdom of God (Matthew 11, 12).*

God is All-knowing. He knows the present and the future. He knows that such and such a person will go to Hell. And that the opposite cannot occur. And many people are concerned about this and question how we can carry on the struggle, given these preconditions. *"Since what the All-knowing Lord knows is bound to happen."*.

Our sinful deeds send us to Hell. And it is we ourselves who commit them. We have free-will. Nobody forces us. Not even God. Somebody steals something? He thinks of it himself, decides for himself and steals by himself. Our actions, our words and our thoughts are controlled by us. We eat, sleep, walk, sin or do good when we want. So, since it is our deeds that send us to Hell and we act of our own accord, then we send ourselves to Hell. That is, it depends on us. Not on the fore-knowledge of God, *"Who desires that all people be saved"* (I Timothy 2, 4).

5. *"Depart further from me, you who are accursed"*.

In the original Greek version of the Bible, the Lord uses a form of the verb which means *"keep on departing"*. That is, those in Hell continue to make their way away from the Lord. They go ever deeper into Hell. They are continuously getting further away from God. *"For they compare that fire to a river, ever flowing in the direction away from God"* (Saint Gregory Palamas, on the Gospel of the Second Coming, 21). As the Righteous in Paradise make progress towards God all the time, so the condition of the sinners in Hell continuously worsens. All the time, they become increasingly estranged from God. In consequence, their torment becomes ever greater.

The same is true of the demons.

16. "I LOOK FOR THE RESURRECTION OF THE DEAD"

1. Harbingers of the Resurrection.

"Young man, I say to you, arise. And the dead man sat up and began to speak and he gave him to his mother" (Luke 7, 15).

Our reasoning faculties are outraged. How did the dead man rise up? But he did not, of his own accord. Christ raised him! And all the dead will arise. Not by themselves or through us who are alive. They will be raised by Christ.

The resurrection of the dead, therefore, is a matter of faith in Christ. Either we believe in Christ, the All-powerful, or *"Little Jesus"*, Who is marginally more powerful than we are ourselves. And that is heresy and blasphemy.

Because of their self-centredness and weakness, people always judge subjectively. One group of people, among those some who are Christians, has no hesitation in linking this sick subjectivity even to God Himself. And they say: *"Is it possible for the dead to rise up? Since they have themselves no power to do so"*. Of course, they are right. It is humanly impossible. For God, on the other hand, it is possible. *"And suppose they are raised"*, they say, *"how is possible for them all to be accommodated, where will they all fit?"* The same mistake here. They equate God with Man. Whether or not everyone will find a place in the next world is not a matter for the Minister of the Environment, but for God Himself. And God is All-powerful. He can give each and every one of us an entire universe. So what if there are billions and billions of people? The same number of universes. What else does *"All-powerful"* mean?

Let us wonder at the power of God. How did this vast world come into existence? The plants, trees, stars, sun, insects, birds, fish, the deep-sea creatures and so on. They came about solely by His word. It did not tire God! And so, this God Himself, Who made this boundless and mysterious universe from nothing and without breaking into a sweat, this God will, at His Second Coming, create some other world. Not from nothing. And consequently with greater ease. This is what is meant by the resurrection of corpses.

And the resurrection of the dead is not a matter for the age to come, but of this one and of the past. It was and is performed not only by Christ Himself but also by His Servants. Both in the Old and New Testaments. And in the Apostolic Age and since then.

Let us examine it further:

The Prophet Elijah in Zarephath of Sidon raised from the dead the son of the widow at whose house he was staying *(I Kings 17)*. The Prophet Elisha raised the dead son of the Shunnamite widow *(II Kings 4)*. The Apostle Peter did likewise to the dead Tabitha *(Acts 9, 40)*.

Abbas Milesios raised a dead person through his prayers.

130

Saint Sisoes resurrected a dead child.

Saint John the Faster, although dead, *"rose and kissed the Eparch Neilos, who had gone to embrace the dead man, according to custom, and exchanged certain words with him, much to the amazement of those present"(The Rudder, ibid.).*

Saint Markianos was extremely charitable. At nights he would roam the streets of Constantinople, seeking an abandoned corpse. If he did, he would wash it and dress it in new clothes, as if it were that of a close relative and would be overjoyed. *"And when he had performed all the duties enjoined on us for the dead, then he would speak to the Corpse as if it were alive.*

- Come, then, brother, he would say to it. Let's exchange the embrace in Christ. At these words - what a dread miracle! - the dead person would come alive again momentarily and kiss the good Markianos "(Εὐεργετινός, vol. III, p. 592).

The following event is even more impressive:

In the year 252 A.D., in the reign of Decius, seven young men from Ephesus were shut up in a cave. Their response was: *"Better to die than to fall into the hands of Decius"*. Decius ordered the cave to be sealed. So that they would die. Later, in 446, during the reign of Theodosius the Younger, a heresy began to spread: disbelief in the resurrection of the dead. Even bishops disbelieved. The Emperor begged the Lord most fervently to provide a solution. And the Lord gave the following sign: He raised up those young men who had been walled up in the cave in Ephesus for one hundred and ninetyfour (194) years! Their bodies, moreover, were completely uncorrupted. As were their clothes. Just as if they had been asleep for a few hours. One of them, Iamblichos, went down into the town of

Ephesus to buy food. Thus it was that the miracle was revealed. And the whole world was shaken to its foundations. This event is celebrated by the Church on 4 August. *"On the fourth day of this month, the memory of the seven young men of Ephesus..."* (Menaion for August, where the relevant narrative is to be found).

2. The Glory of the Bodies.

a. Their brightness.

To what extent did Christ shine on Mount Tabor? *"And his face shone like the sun"* (Matthew 19, 2). Like the sun! As Christ shone on Tabor, so did Adam in Paradise. And so shall the righteous shine in the age to come. And as much glory as Christ had on Tabor, so had Adam in Paradise, and so shall the righteous have in the age to come *(Saint Gregory Palamas)*.

The righteous have already enjoyed such glory on earth. Moses, for example, and the blessed Pambo, Silouan, Sisoes, Seraphim of Sarov. Why do they shine? When a metal is pure, it radiates. Not by itself, because it has no light. The sun has light. And the sun sends light onto the metal. And since it is pure, it receives the light and reflects it. The same is true of the righteous. Their souls radiate, but not of their own accord. Because they do not have their own light. The Lord is Light. And the Lord enlightens the soul. And since it is pure, it receives the light. So, it shines *(Saint Kallistos, Philokalia)*.

And virtue is light. *"Let us put on the armour of light"* (Romans 13, 12), that is, the virtues. Thus, when we perform works of virtue, we store up light inside ourselves. At the Second Coming of Christ, all our works will be made plain. Words, recollections, deeds. And the works of virtue, as light, shine.

Now the light simply accumulates within us. The glory. In the age to come, that light will be manifested and strengthened. It is like winter and spring. In winter, nature seems dead. But the mechanics by which nature blossoms are silently at work. And in spring, nature flowers. It blossoms in spring because during the winter the measures preparatory for this flourishing were being taken. So it is with souls. Now, in the winter, the good, the glory, the light is silently being accumulated. And they will be revealed in the spring, in the next age.

Whatever people sow, they reap. Whatever they have laid up in their souls, this will be revealed, will express itself in the body in the last times. And sin is darkness! *(Romans 13,12)*.

It follows that the bodies of the sinners will be raised as black as pitch. The righteous will be white, like the Sun, and will give off the fragrance of the grace of the Holy Spirit. And the sinners will be black as pitch and will reek of the stench of sin!

b. Pleasure.

Adam in Paradise had one form of pleasure: enjoyment of the divine beauty. With his fall, this pleasure changed momentum; from the divine, it became earthly, fleshly, sinful *(cf. Saint Maximos, Century 6, 33)*. So the multifarious pleasures which people now taste (gluttony, sins of the flesh and so on), are the perversion of divine pleasure, of the joy of Paradise which the First-created felt.

When people are cleansed, enlightened, sanctified,

that pleasure reassumes its original form. It becomes divine pleasure. And then all earthly pleasures are no more than dregs for them *(Philippians 3, 19)*. They are so transformed that, for instance, they are no longer aware of food; that is, whether or not they have eaten. We read in the Sayings of the Fathers that the disciple of Saint Sisoes would often say to him: *"Abbas, come. Let's eat"*. And the saint would ask him: *"Haven't we eaten, my child?"* *"No, father"*. *"Well, if we haven't, bring something and let's do so"*. And besides, Saint Sisoes would go and take communion even though he had eaten, just like a little child! He forgot that he had eaten. *"I further believe that the food they eat gives them no satisfaction"*, says the Blessed John of Sinai *(The Ladder, ibid., Logos 30, 11)*.

The Apostle Paul says: *"Food is for the stomach and the stomach for food - and God will do away with both the one and the other" (I Corinthians 6, 13)*. This does not mean that people will be without stomachs! Simply that in the age to come there will be no desire for nor any pleasure in food. Which is why God will also do away with this (food).

Multifarious pleasures are the fruit of sin. And pain the product of pleasure. This is why there will be no pain in the age to come. Precisely because there will be no pleasure as the fruit of sin. Neither sorrow, nor sighing but life everlasting.

c. The undeniable passions.

The undeniable passions (tiredness, pain, thirst, hunger, sleep, cowardice, fear, cold, sorrow etc.) which also formed part of the human nature of the Lord will be rooted out from people in the age to come by death.

They are already rooted out in this age in those who have been transfigured. As a prelude to their future and infinite transformation. Let us look at this more closely.

The Prophet Isaiah foretells: *"But those who await the Lord shall renew their strength... they shall run and not grow tired, walk and not grow hungry"* (Isaiah 40, 31). The experience of Saint John of Sinai confirms this. *"Those who have attained this degree (of love) equal to the angels' often forget all about bodily food. And I believe that they do not want it so frequently, which is not at all improbable, since even desire which is not from God often takes away the appetite for food"*. Saint Isaak the Syrian confirms this: *"They say of one bird, the siren, that whoever hears its melodic song will be so overwhelmingly attracted by it that they will be completely taken up by the sweetness of the song and will forget about the necessities of life. They collapse, at death's door, because of the intoxication brought about by the sheer pleasure of this song. The same effect can be observed in the soul when it receives the action of love... Then, under the sway and domination of this pleasure, the body is deadened towards its impulses, not only those which are unnatural, but even those which are perfectly natural, which are inborn, such as hunger, thirst and so on"* (Εὐεργετινός, vol. IV, p. 85)

Nor is it only that the bodies of the saints do not feel hunger and thirst to the same extent, but that they do not fall ill so easily. *"I believe that even the bodies of those who have reached such a state of incorruption do not fall ill so easily, because in a way they have now been purified and made incorruptible. That is to say that the flame of purity has extinguished that of the bodily passions and sicknesses"*

(The Ladder, ibid.).

But the bodies of the saints do not even feel pain! How was it possible for some of the holy martyrs to undergo such fearsome torments with total calm, peace, tranquillity and joy? Did they not have bodies? And when the body is injured, does it not hurt? And the more it is injured, does it not suffer the greater?

This is the miracle. And miracles are performed by God, not people. The fact that they felt no pain is due to their willingness to suffer torments for the sake of the Lord and to the outpouring of Divine Grace onto the bodies of the martyrs. To put it more simply. If someone has an operation, they are given anaesthetic. Even though their bodies are cut open by the surgeon's knife, they do not feel anything because of the anaesthetic. The same is true of the martyrs. Their bodies were *"drugged"* by the deluge of Divine Grace. By the passionate love of God. *"Having been reconstituted, all love, by the Maker you will not feel pain of the body" (ode 4, canon for November 18).* For the same reason, ascetics often do not feel the excessive fatigue caused by their labours, says the Blessed Niketas Stethatos. This is a prelude to the future state of our resurrected bodies.

Where the fact that the undeniable passions are already deadened in this age is most tangible, however, is in the life of Saint Seraphim of Sarov.

"- What else do you feel? ,he asks his disciple Motovilov.

- I'm amazingly warm.

- Warm? What do you mean, my dear fellow? Here we are sitting in the depths of the forest in mid-winter, with snow under our feet and more falling from the sky and settling inch-deep on our clothes. How can you feel warm?

- I feel the same warmth as one does in a hot bath, when they throw water on the stove and a column of steam rises up.

- You've just told me that all around us it is as warm as in a hot bath. And yet look. The snow that's settled on us isn't melting and it's continuing to fall from the sky. That means that the warmth isn't in the air, but inside us...It was with this that hermits, men and women, were able to disdain the winter frost. They felt as if they were dressed in warm furs..." (The Life of Saint Seraphim).

These undeniable passions, therefore, have already been anaesthetised in this life. How much more so will they be in the age to come? So the body in the next life will be without the undeniable passions, it will be a different body, a *"spiritual"* one (I Corinthians 15, 44).

d. "they will take wing like eagles"

"But those who await the Lord will renew their strength, they shall take wing like eagles" (Isaiah 40, 31). The righteous will fly like eagles. And they will walk on the waters of the seas and rivers as if on dry land. Like Christ on the Lake of Gennesaret. That is to say that the grace of the Lord will elevate the bodies. It will endow them with super-natural qualities. Just as the risen Body of the Lord had. Although *"the tomb was sealed"*, He came out. He went into the house of His disciples, *"the doors being locked"*. The bodies of the righteous will be just like that: *"imperturbable, impassive, unsubstantial, like the body of the Lord passing through doors after the Resurrection"* (Saint Cyril of Jerusalem, P.G. vol. 33, 1040).

EPILOGUE

Ignorance of what happens after death is no excuse. That will not save us.

Suppose there is some food containing poison and, without knowing, we eat it. Will we not be poisoned? Of course we will. Ignorance will not prevent it. In the same way, ignorance of our end is not an extenuating circumstance to gain us exemption from the toll-houses, nor the judgement, nor Hell. We would do well to find out...

Knowledge of the last things is beneficial to the soul. *"In all you do, remember the end of your life and you will never sin" (Wisdom of Sirach 7, 36)*. The famous ascetic Evagrius relates: *"I have seen many who, with these thoughts, obtained many tears and cleansed their spiritual powers in a most wonderful way"*. Abbas Evagrius advises: *"When you're sitting in your cell, collect your thoughts. Remember the day of death. Look at the necrosis of the body then. Feel that great horror. Accept the labour. Realise the vanity of the world. In that way, you'll always be intent on quietude and you won't fall ill. Recollect what the souls are like there, in what most terrible silence, in what most bitter sighing and in what fear and anguish and apprehension. The* unceasing pain. The spiritual, unquenchable tears".

"But remember also the day of the Resurrection, when we shall stand before God. Imagine that dreadful and terrible Seat of Judgement. Bring to the fore what awaits those who sin. The enormous shame in the face of God, the Angels, the Archangels and the whole of mankind. That is to say punishments, eternal fire, the worm which never sleeps, the bowels of the earth, the darkness, the gnashing of teeth, the terrors and the torments".

"Think now of the good things which await the righteous, the boldness of speech they will enjoy in the face of God the Father and His Christ, the Angels and Archangels, the whole assembly of the saints, the kingdom of Heaven, its gifts, its joy and its own special enjoyment. Call to mind both the one group and the other. And weep for the condemnation of the sinners, mourn, in the fear of finding yourself among them. As to those things which await the righteous, rejoice and be glad. Make sure that you enjoy them and become a stranger to the rest. Make it your concern that you never, whether you're in your cell or outside, lose the remembrance of them. In that way, if you keep them in mind, you'll avoid filthy and harmful thoughts".

And he concludes:

"Since this is the way things are, in what manner should we live? In holy reversion to the good, in all piety. What love we must acquire! What conduct and manner of life! What a road! What fervour! What prayer! What surety! In the expectation of all that, let us take good care that we appear before God spotless and immaculate, in peace. So that we shall be found worthy of hearing His voice as He says: Come, you who are blessed by my Father, inherit unto the ages of ages *the kingdom that was prepared for you from the beginning of time".*

Archbishop Theophilos, in his final moments, said: *"How blessed you are, Abbas Arsenios, that you always bore in mind this hour".*

GLOSSARY OF TERMS

Euchologion: Priest's prayer book.

Paraclitic/paraclisis: A canon of intercession to the Mother of God or a Saint.

Holy Anaphora: The central, oblationary, part of the Communion Service.

Menologion/Menaion: Books containing the variable parts of the services for each month.

Philokalia: A collection of writings on spiritual matters, widely used by the Orthodox.

Logos: Homily

Triodion: The service book for Great Lent.

CONTENTS

OTHER ENGLISH EDITIONS
FROM " TERTIOS "

1. **"Your will be done - Orthodoxy in Mission".** Edited by: *Lemopoulos George.*
p. 272, ISBN 2-8254-0951-0

2. **"You shall by my Witnesses".** Edited by: *Lemopoulos George.* Mission stories from the Eastern and Oriental Orthodox Churches.
p. 192, ISBN 960-7297-58-X

ECUMENICAL PATRIARCHATE
3. **"The place of the Woman in the Orthodox Church and the question of the Ordination of Women".**
Interorthodox Symposium, Rhodos, November 1988. A collective volume edited by Gennadios Limouris.
p. 348, ISBN 960-7297-41-5

4. **"The Grace of God sanctifies the Water".**
A book of catechism for children, who can learn while colouring pictures. The texts are both in English and Greek.
Format 21X28, in full colour
p. 64, ISBN 960-7297-63-6

Φωτοστοιχειοθεσία — Ἐκτύπωση Ὄφσετ «ΝΕΑ ΣΤΟΙΧΕΙΟΘΕΤΙΚΗ»
Ἀχελώου 6 — Τηλ. (031) 542.940 - 522.503 — ΘΕΣΣΑΛΟΝΙΚΗ

Π. Γιαννούλης - Κ. Τσολερίδης